LONG-RANGE PLANNING FOR YOUR BUSINESS

LONG-RANGE PLANNING FOR YOUR BUSINESS:

An Operating Manual

Merritt L. Kastens

A Division of American Management Associations

Library of Congress Cataloging in Publication Data

Kastens, Merritt L
  Long-range planning for your business.

  Includes bibliographical references and index.
  1. Business--Handbooks, manuals, etc. 2. Plan-
ning--Handbooks, manuals, etc. I. Title.
HF5353.K32   658.4'01   75-41378
ISBN 0-8144-5413-5

© 1976 AMACOM
A division of American Management Associations, New York. All rights reserved. Printed in the United States of America.

Second Printing

To Kim
whose plans seldom work out
but always are successful

Preface

WHY another book on planning? Simply because clients and manager friends are continually asking me, "But how do you *do* planning?" The literature on planning mostly tells you how to "think about" planning, but it does not say much about the operations, the manipulations, the actions that actually constitute a planning procedure. This bias is probably due in part to the fact that most of the books are intended to be used sometimes in a classroom. Now, you cannot *do* business planning in a classroom. You do not have either the inputs or the judgment—even with good case studies. You can *think* about planning in a classroom, and master the principles and concepts.

Most literature on general management problems seems to suffer from this remoteness from the point of application. It is not simply a matter of polarization between theorists and practitioners because practicing managers frequently write in this detached style also. The hiatus seems to be caused by a missing link in communications media.

So this book is styled as an "Operating Manual" in the hope that it will bridge the gap by giving explicit directions for operating a planning procedure. In taking this approach, I accept the fact that it contains certain inherent deficiencies. A good planning process is tailor-made to the characteristics and problems of a specific organization. No one formula works for everybody. However, if this book were to attempt to discuss all the options, all the possible sideloops, all the conditional responses, it would be very long and extremely difficult to follow. So it takes a single sequence of critical planning steps that together make up a complete planning cycle. It is a rather simple cycle in order that it will have the broadest possible applicability and be practical for relatively small organizations.

The procedure is spread out over a 12-month period, not that there is any magic to a year-long cycle. The yearly process does seem to be a kind of natural rhythm, however. It synchronizes with the budget cycle and the seasonality that affects some businesses. It is hard to produce a plan in less time anyway: first, because it would require large blocs of executive time within a few months and second, because you need time to complete the information gathering and analyses that provide the planting inputs. If you stretch your planning process beyond a year, the work done in the beginning phases may become obsolete before the job is complete, and you can find yourself continually recycling and reworking.

The examples given here imply a five-year plan. There is no magic to that particular planning horizon either. It is very commonly used, and it fits into the figures handily, but you may need a longer or a shorter period in your particular circumstances. You may have to experiment to find out what is the proper "long range" for you.

To those who would propose a different emphasis or include steps that have been omitted, I can only say *pace*. Of course there are other ways to do it, and some will be more fruitful in any given circumstance. But, just as you can't learn to ride a bicycle by reading a book, the best way to learn how to design *your* ideal planning process is to try this one and find out where you can gain real control over your destiny and where the effort seems to be excessive. Then you can write your own operating manual.

Some management terms have been used in a special, limited way—*policy*, for instance—and some have been consciously avoided. This was done to keep the vocabulary simple, and implies no attempt to redefine any terms. If you know other definitions, table them until you finish the book. Management terminology is pretty chaotic anyway, and nobody is going to learn anything by a hassle over lexicography.

The cycle presented here is the distillation of many different planning systems that I have helped design for large- and small-company clients. Those managements deserve to be recognized for their contribution to this book by experimenting with me on different sequences, different procedures, even different nomenclatures. It is to their further credit that most of them are still experimenting—that is, still learning. I also must acknowledge the inestimable contributions of my live-in editor, Anita S. Kastens, and my indefatigable typist, Audrey J. Snyder.

Merritt L. Kastens

Contents

1
Planning for Leadership

Planning is . . . attending to the goals we ought to be thinking about and never do, the facts we do not like to face and the questions we lack the courage to ask.
JOHN GARDNER

BY this time every manager has heard a thousand times that planning is the key to growth and security in operating a business. Planning saves time. Planning assures that corporate resources are used where they can do the most good. Planning minimizes the crisis-to-crisis atmosphere of reactive management. Planning is good for you.

Unfortunately, like so many things that are good for you, it seems difficult to get around to actually doing it. Most managers hear about the elaborate planning staffs of the corporate giants with their systems analysts, operations analysts, business analysts, market analysts, and planning coordinators, and they despair of duplicating these functions in a smaller organization. They also hear that the line manager must be his or her own chief planning officer and wonder how in heaven's name it is possible to take on all this activity in addition to the already substantial demands on his or her time. As a consequence, only too frequently they throw up their hands in despair, or at best they call in subordinates and say, "Hey, I'd like you to make some long-range plans this year and have them in to me by the end of the year." Result: The company drifts on pretty much as it always has, hopefully keeping its head above water but with no forceful strategic direction.

Of course, if you are content to go along the way you always have, you don't need a plan. You don't need a plan to tell you to keep doing what you have always done. It would be a waste of time. Planning implies change. It is the companies operating in the most rapidly changing environments, with high technological obsolescence and unstable markets, that do the most elaborate planning. They have to. They need a conscious mechanism to force themselves to reexamine their activities continually and to commit themselves to new ways of pursuing their businesses. Stagnation would be suicide. Companies in more stable industries, where there is plenty of time to react to changing circumstances, have not felt the urgency to plan for change. However, there are fewer and fewer such stable industries with each passing year.

Be sure that everyone you involve in a planning process understands this correlation between planning and change. Some people are not going to like it and will resist planning for all sorts of ostensible reasons. Don't be surprised. They don't want to change. They got a good job doing what they did in the past. Why take a chance? You are going to have to fight this attitude—or at least counteract it—with all the interpersonal skills you can muster. And you will probably lose sometimes. Well, in almost any organization there are jobs that do not require strategic conceptualizing, where circumstances don't change very much, where good tight scheduling is all that is needed. But you can't lead anything if you are standing still.

Then again, you may have the other problem: a bunch of butterfly chasers riding off in all directions after the grass on the other side of the fence. Change is not just for change's sake. You want a plan that will insure a stable platform from which you can launch meaningful changes at a rate and to an extent your resources can support. The discipline imposed by formal planning—if you insist on it—can keep your gunslingers in check, reduce the waste of resources on half-baked schemes, and prevent you from initiating more innovations at one time than you can possibly support.

You are going to involve a lot of people in your strategic plan, but they will have to work within some kind of overall framework for the total enterprise or most of their efforts will be wasted. "Participative management" is not just fancy jargon for "passing the buck." The best way to build a strategic framework is from the top down, not for any theoretical reason but simply because it works. "Bottom-up" planning schemes provoke all the frustrations of pushing on a rope. They take a lot of time, often produce a lot of unhappy people, and seldom result in anything being done that would not have been done anyway. Anyone who has any working experience with planning knows this, but the theorists are still arguing about it. Leaders must lead, and the place for leadership is in setting the trajectory, not in making the midcourse corrections.

Strategic planning, if it is to be done at all well, must begin with the chief executive officer and proceed down through the leadership structure—which is to say, through the "line" structure. This is no less true in a large company than in a small one, although it gets more difficult in a large company. Presumably this is why presidents of large companies get paid more than presidents of small ones.

Strategic planning is the mechanism for exercising leadership, and therefore it must be done by the people who expect to lead, not by the rear-echelon support troops. It is going to require a commitment of time. However, if adequate time is not allocated, the planning job is not going to get done; so it behooves any manager with presumptions of leadership to make the time. Unless the manager has been slacking somewhere, that means some other activities will have to be delegated. So be it! One of the principal fruits of good planning is to allocate your resources where they have the most impact. If you do not think that leadership is one of your most important responsibilities, perhaps you should reallocate the time you expected to spend reading the rest of this book.

The time requirement need not be terribly burdensome. What the responsible manager must contribute are the judgmental, decision-making inputs. This is tough, sweaty work; don't think it is easy. But if you don't do it, it won't get done. You cannot delegate it. Those large planning staffs in the big companies gather facts and make analyses. If you have such staff support, fine; but this work can be done through ad hoc assignments within the organization or by outside services.

Planning must be based on good, sound, factual information, but remember, in this unsettled world you need to provide a margin for error even with the best possible data. Long-range strategic decisions are usually based on data with a reliability of no more than plus-or-minus 25 percent. Get the facts, and be sure they are honest facts and not wishful dreams, but you don't have to massage them into a pulp in a high-capacity computer in order to make up your mind what you want to do.

It is entirely feasible for you, with the resources at your disposal, to control the destiny of the activities for which you have managerial and leadership responsibility. This book presents a stripped-down sequence of steps that will enable you to make up your mind just where you want to go, what is the best way to get there, and what to do to start making things happen so that the future turns out the way you would like it to turn out.

The procedure has been stripped down to make it practicable for small companies, which arbitrarily means around $100 million or less in annual sales these days. However, it is a good starting point for larger companies, too. No matter what your size, once you have mastered the skeleton you will want to decorate it with more sophisticated techniques. Don't rush it. Experienced planners agree that it takes about five planning cycles before an organization begins to feel comfortable and competent in long-range planning. One of the reasons it takes so long is that most outfits try to do too much too soon.

This book is primarily addressed to chief executive officers. As a convenience in expression, the text will often refer to the CEO; but, remember, every responsible manager is chief executive officer in the sense that he is primarily responsible for critical decisions regarding the development of a certain area of activity delegated to his responsibility and for the optimum disposition of certain physical, financial, and human resources entrusted to his stewardship. If your area of responsibility is limited, you may find that you can further compress some of the steps described here, but don't skip any step.

Furthermore, the book is written for managers who can delegate responsibility and hold their subordinates accountable for results. If you are willing to accept interminable alibis and can be conned into accepting performance substantially below what you expected, you have wasted your money buying this book and you will waste your time reading it.

This book will not make you any smarter. If you have lousy judgment, all it will do is enable you to make mistakes in an orderly fashion. If you are given to self-deluding pipe dreams, you are going to fall on your face no matter how elegantly those pipe dreams have been conceptualized. If you do not know how to handle your people and try to impose your perceptions on them arbitrarily without their full understanding or concurrence, your plans will not materialize. But, given those caveats, you can establish a sense of direction in your enterprise and provide a central rationale to which current decisions can be related and against which progress can be measured. This is a lot to accomplish even if it does not guarantee instant fame and fortune. It is not all that difficult, so let us get on with the job.

We are going to assume that you are starting your planning cycle in January to provide a time line for the various steps. Of course that is a convention of convenience. You can start your planning process at any time that is most convenient in terms of your fiscal year, commercial season, and vacation schedule. Figures 1 and 2 provide an approximate 12-month

Figure I. Typical planning calendar.

Month	Days	Function	People Involved						
			CEO	Exec. VP	Fin. VP	Sales VP	Prod. VP	Res. VP	Other
January	1	Mission	X	X	X	X	X	X	?
January	1	Strategic policies	X	X	X	X	X	X	?
January	?	Request market analysis				X			X
February	½	Competitive analysis	X		X	X	X	X	
February	1	Environmental analysis	X	X	X	X	X	X	X
February	?	Request action plans for threats and opportunities						X	X
March	1	Operation analysis	X	X	X		X	X	
March	?	Assign projects to correct weaknesses							X
March	?	Assign projects to exploit strengths							X
March		Market analysis due				X			
March	1	Primary objectives	X	X	X	X	X	X	
March	?	Assign development objectives for programming	X						
April	½	Approve and implement, or defer, plans to meet threats	X	X	?	?	?	?	
April	½	Review and approve plans for opportunities.	X	X	?	?	?	?	
May	½	Approve and implement plans for weaknesses	X	X	?	?	?	?	
May	½	Review and approve plans for strengths	X	X	?	?	?	?	
June	1	Marketing plan presentation	X	X	X	X	X	X	
July	½-1	Facilities plan presentation	X	X	X		X	X	
August	½	Profit forecast I	X	X	X				
September	2	Presentation of development objectives programs	X	X	X	X	X	X	X
October	½	Profit forecast II	X	X	X				
October	½-1	Profitability plan	X	X	X	X	X	X	
November		Detailed plans completed			X	X	X	X	X
December	1	Summary meeting	X	X	X	X	X	X	X

Figure 2. Typical planning schedule.

Function	Jan.	Feb.	Mar.	Apr.	May	June	July	Aug.	Sept.	Oct.	Nov.	Dec.	Jan.
Mission meeting	▓												
Policy meeting	▓												
Market analysis		▓	▓										
Competitive analysis		▓											
Environmental analysis		▓	▓										
Prepare action plans, threats, and opportunities			▓										
Operations analysis			▓										
Prepare action plans, weaknesses				▓									
Prepare action plans, strengths				▓	▓								
Primary objectives meeting			▓										
Program development objectives						▓	▓	▓					
Prepare marketing plan					▓	▓							
Prepare facilities plan					▓	▓							
Profit forecast I							▓						
Profit forecast II								▓					
Prepare detailed plans									▓	▓			
Summary meeting											▓		
Market analysis													▓

NOTE: *Shaded bars indicate approximate duration of the task.*

calendar and schedule. You will want to refer to them from time to time.

Get yourself a loose-leaf binder to use as a planning book and provide one for everybody else as you involve them in the planning process. A binder one-inch thick should be big enough. If you generate more backup papers than you can get into that size, put them in a separate book so that you can keep the main structure of the developing plan highly visible.

The written record of your plan is most important because one of the big things you expect from your planning effort is the assurance that everyone has the same notion of what is going on, and why. Furthermore, you want to make sure that six months or a year from now nobody forgets just why you started a given project in the first place. To accomplish this communication, you have to write down plans, but more than that, you have to write them down specifically and unambiguously. If the statements are vague, you can expect the actions to be vague. If there is any possibility of ambiguity, you can count on someone's reading it the "wrong" way should this suit his or her personal interest. So start right at the beginning to learn how to be a hard-nosed editor. Be sure you "say what you mean and mean what you say." This is a fundamental technique to be mastered if your planning is to be effective. We will say much more about planning books as we go along, but you may as well get started right.

SUGGESTED READING

Anonymous, *Planning for Future Company Growth: A Small Company Must,* File 32. New York: Research Institute of America, 1967.

Just what the title says it is.

Ansoff, H. I., et al., "Does Planning Pay?" *Long-Range Planning,* Vol. 3, No. 2 (December 1970).

Reports the effect of planning on the success of acquisitions.

Arnold, J. D., "The Chin-Down Manager," *Fortune,* Vol. 90, No. 1 (July 1974), pp. 98–99.

"Can anything be done for the chin-down manager? Can he be saved? He has to be saved because he is all of us and there is no one else. But . . . he will have to overcome fears and take risks."

Drucker, P. W., *The Effective Executive.* New York: Harper & Row, 1966–1967. See especially, pp. 25–51.

"I have yet to see an executive, regardless of rank or station, who could not consign something like a quarter of the demands on his time to the wastebasket without anybody's noticing their disappearance." If you can't manage time, you can't manage anything.

Ewing, D. W., *The Human Side of Planning.* New York: The Macmillan Company, 1969.

A whole book on why people resist planning. It cites P. H. Meyers' study of planning practices in a number of companies. The CEO's of the most successful companies in terms of growth in sales and profits reported that they spent from 500 to 1,000 hours in planning meetings during the year. The CEO of the least successful company estimated that he spent 30 hours at that sort of thing.

Foster, D., "Planning in the Smaller Company," *Long-Range Planning,* Vol. 4, No. 3 (September 1971), pp. 71–81.

Detailed description of a rather elaborate planning process for a small company. It does cover all the points, even though you may not want to use them.

Herold, D. M., "Long-Range Planning and Organizational Performance," *Academy of Management Journal* (March 1972).

Compares the profit and sales performance of companies with formal planning systems and informal planning in the drug and chemical industry. The formal planners do better in both good years and bad years.

Jones, H., *Preparing Company Plans*. New York: Halsted Press, 1974.

Another approach to business planning.

Kastens, M. L., "Who Does the Planning?" *Managerial Planning*, Vol. 20, No. 4 (January–February 1972).

Why the line officers must exercise planning responsibility and what planning staffs can do.

MacKenzie, R. A., *The Time Trap* (AMACOM, 1972).

If you really want to get your time schedule in hand, here is the book for you. Should save you 20 to 25 percent of your day.

Mace, M. L., "The President and Corporate Planning," *Harvard Business Review*, Vol. 43, No. 1 (January–February 1965).

A classic! By all means read it.

Steiglitz, H., *The Chief Executive—And His Job*. New York: The Conference Board, 1969.

In a survey of 280 CEO's, 65 percent of the respondents designated long-range planning as their most important activity, and they reported that they spent an average of 44 percent of their time on it. They may have been bragging.

Thune, S. S., and House, R. J., "Where Long-Range Planning Pays Off," *Business Horizons*, Vol. 13 (August 1970).

Reports a study of 67 companies in which formal planning is practiced. Performance after planning was introduced is compared with an equal period of time preplanning. On the average, they had 38 percentage points greater sales increase, 64 percentage points greater earnings per share, and 56 percentage points greater appreciation in stock price in the planned period than they had had in the equal period before planning. In another comparison, performance of 71 companies using formal planning is measured against performance of 21 "informal" planners in their own industry. The "planners" outperformed the "informal" planners by 44 percent in growth in earnings per share, 38 percent in return on equity, and 32 percent in return on total capital employed. The planners also outperformed the nonplanners in sales growth and stock-price appreciation, but for technical reasons these last data were not believed to be statistically rigorous.

Vancil, Richard F., and Lorange, Peter, "Strategic Planning in Diversified Companies," *Harvard Business Review,* Vol. 53, No. 1 (January–February 1975).

Additional planning procedures for divisionalized companies.

2

What Do You Think You're Doing?

CALL it mission, charter, purpose, role, definition of the business. The question is: What business do you choose to be in? In what arena do you propose to compete? If you don't know what game you are playing, there is no way to decide whether you should run, dribble, or putt. It is a tough question because you do have so much freedom of choice. No book can tell you what the answer should be. It's an important question because probably no other single decision will have so much impact in determining how fast, how far, and how soundly your enterprise will grow. Take some time for it.

Block out a half day, a day, a week if necessary in which you will entertain no consideration other than this basic question. A day should normally be amply sufficient. If it takes longer, this is the best possible evidence that the sense of direction of the enterprise has been muddled and that it is vitally important to decide for once just what sort of a beast you are. Get away from your office and find a comfortable place where you can phone out for information but where no phone calls can get in. Commit yourself to staying locked up until you finally make up your mind: no breaks for golf, no recesses for "critical" side conferences on other subjects. Get yourself a big chalkboard so that you can draft and redraft until you know exactly what you are saying.

Whom do you take with you for this kind of session? The people whose judgment you respect in determining the future destiny of the enterprise. I don't know who they are. They may be other corporate officers; they may be board members; they may include your general counsel, your research director. The point is: Do not be hamstrung by your organization chart. Do not be "polite." If there is no one whose judgment you trust in matters of this importance, go off by yourself. If you choose to do it solo, it will be quick, but solo decisions run the risk of being narrow. The more people you involve, the broader the perspective you will get, but the more time it's going to take to come to a conclusion. Decision time doesn't quite increase proportionately to the number of people involved, but there is a strong correlation.

Define Your Market

When you get locked into the conference room, what do you do? Well, you know what you are good at. You have mastered a certain kind of process or fabrication. You have access to certain markets or marketing channels. You are hotshots in a certain field of technology or maybe at manipulating balance sheets. You have a wide reputation for fulfilling a certain kind of function like making hand tools or transporting freight or conveying goods around inside a building. Okay, that's fine; but what are you going to do with this outstanding capability? No matter how you see yourself from inside the organization, there is no business until somebody buys something. You must look outside to introduce a sense of reality into your strategies. You are going to provide a certain kind of goods or services *to a certain group of customers*—a certain market. Define that market right in the mission statement so that it has operational significance in the way you manage the company. If you manufacture shoes, are you going to manufacture all kinds of shoes, or dress shoes, or sports shoes, or men's shoes, or women's shoes, or work shoes? Are you going to distribute them nationally, internationally, regionally?

How do you decide? There are some pretty good rules of thumb. Define your product/service against a market in which you can see at least a 10 percent share in a reasonable time span. Since you have the power of decision in determining just what should be the scope of your production, and also free choice as to how you segment the market, this is not so difficult as it might seem at first blush. If you cannot be a significant factor in the total product line, concentrate on the high quality or the custom segment of the market. If you can't be a power in your business nationally, do not scatter your shots all over the landscape: Concentrate on a regional market.

In most businesses, if you do not have 10 percent of the market, you are going to have to live on table scraps. You will be vulnerable to being squeezed out. You are going to have a tough time keeping up with the competitive pace in marketing effort, in research backup, in customer service, and in keeping your image before the customers. Why make it hard for yourself?

On the other hand, if you define your mission in such a fashion that you are getting up toward 50 percent of the market, you will run into other kinds of problems. Of course, if demand is growing at such a vigorous rate that you have trouble expanding just to keep up with the natural growth, by all means ride your winner as long and as hard as you can. But in the more usual situation, you begin to run out of scope for expansion at this point. Traditionally, the market share of the dominant competitor in a stable, slow-growing market turns out to be 50 percent. Don't ask me why; it just is. Very often part of the second 50 percent of the market is captive or is subject to special situations or special requirements that make it harder to penetrate. A competitive product innovation or a price war hurts you more than it does anyone else. Better broaden your sights. Don't give up any sales that you are making now, but it is time to look for contiguous fields to conquer.

Of course, if you have a truly new product or service for which there is no established market, these kinds of benchmarks are relatively meaningless. However, this sort of problem really arises only in a new venture and is not the kind of situation that a going concern is likely to be involved in.

One very important concept about mission statements: Mission statements are directive, not proscriptive. They set the direction of central thrust. They do not exclude any kind of opportunistic activity that might land in your lap. If you decide to concentrate on national markets, it does not mean that you should turn down some marginal export sales if the opportunity arises. If you are determined to make it or break it in the work-shoe market, you are not going to ignore the fact that college kids may buy your shoes for sport shoes. Your mission statement tells you where you are going to concentrate your resources, where you are going to look hardest for new opportunities, where you are going to try to build the success of the enterprise. It says nothing about possible opportunities that may arise on the periphery of your central interest, other than to warn that you don't intend to consciously build off on any of these tangents.

In defining your business, you can take a number of different points of view. None of them is particularly right or wrong. The one you choose will reflect your assessment of the relative strengths of your organization and, to a certain extent, your own preferences—where you feel the most comfortable.

The Raw-Materials-Based Company

Let us consider, for example, a relatively integrated food-processing company, which might, for instance, declare:

> The business of the XYZ Company is to convert grain into useful products for the world market.

In this case the company is a grain converter; it does things to a certain kind of raw material—grind it, or ferment it, or extract it, or react it chemically. It may make industrial products, food product components, or finished consumer products; but the emphasis is on the material that is processed. Back in the days when CPC International was the Corn Products Company, the managers undoubtedly perceived themselves in this way. A. E. Staley and Company still does. So did most of the big oil companies until quite recently, although the raw material involved is quite different. Now, of course, most of them quite reasonably have declared themselves in the "energy" business as their raw material base has gotten chancy. A lot of them are having trouble effecting this reorientation, too, because that is just not the way their executives were brought up.

The strategic thrust of a materials-oriented company is going to be toward getting the raw material cheaper, finding additional products that can be made out of the raw material, and looking for ways to realize greater total profit out of the material, possibly through forward integration. It may have trouble fulfilling the 10 percent share-of-market (SOM) rule, but if you look at the multinational oil companies or the big grain companies, you can see the relationship between profitability and SOM.

The Process Company

However, another apparently quite similar company might say that its mission is:

> . . . to develop and produce baked goods for the national home consumer market.

Here the emphasis is on the processing technology. This company will use any kind of raw material (sawdust, conceivably) to make any kind of consumer product—bread, cookies, breakfast food, instant pastries, dog food—as long as it goes through a bakery. It will probably try to be a leader in oven technology, have the lowest possible processing cost, and strive mightily to inject baked products into markets currently served by other kinds of food products—pretzels versus popcorn, for instance. A couple of generations ago, a lot of flour millers ultimately made the transition from a raw materials orientation to one of consumer product production (bakers), and some subsequently even stopped milling flour altogether.

The companies that consider themselves "manufacturing chemists" are process-oriented; they will consider any business venture in which their chemical process technology might be applicable. Most electronics companies bet on their ability to make money by exploiting their electronics technology capability, regardless of the materials used or the market served. You have to be big to bring this one off—like a Du Pont, for instance—or define your process field very narrowly, as in the case of E. H. Titchner & Company of Binghamton, N.Y., which concentrates on precision wire bending and welding. A lot of small, self-proclaimed "electronics" companies came to grief because they failed to realize this. In general, the ones that saw themselves as manufacturers of "choppers," or potentiometers, or cathode-ray tubes did better.

The Marketing Company

From both the previous instances you may reasonably infer that production and engineering types are calling the shots—in fact, they had better be! If they are not, the company is going to get itself into trouble. But if marketing people are setting the strategy, they are apt to decide that the mission of the XYZ Company is:

> . . . to develop, manufacture, and market packaged consumer food products under franchised brands in the United States and in advanced market countries abroad.

The people in marketing don't care what the products are made of. They don't care how they are made. They do want them in a package, and they do want to sell them on the basis of brand recognition. Obviously they think they are good at developing new products, establishing (franchising) brand recognition, and getting the products out into the distribution channels. They do say "food products," though; so, except for incidental items, they intend to stay in the food business. They could have said "nutrition," but unless they changed the rest of the statement (and the meaning), it wouldn't do anything but fuzzle-up the language.

Most of the major diversified food companies follow this kind of strategy. But so do A. B. Dick with copying equipment, Eastman Kodak with cameras, Babcock and Wilcox with power equipment. They supply a certain kind of product to meet a certain segment of market demand, and they are extremely flexible about where the product comes from. They may even have the product custom-packed for them, although from the language used here, you would expect that they would plan to eventually produce it themselves.

The Distribution Company

If the XYZ Company is selling-oriented rather than marketing-oriented, the management may decide that the business is to:

> . . . supply branded consumer products to mass retail food-merchandising organizations wherever such organizations exist.

Management is essentially saying that the company can sell to supermarkets better than anybody, and it does not matter whether it is corn flakes, or soap powder, or antiperspirant, or games it is selling. Obviously the strategy is going to be much different from that in any of the preceding examples. Lockheed has this kind of commitment to a specific channel of distribution as a supplier to the defense/space establishment. It knows how to sell government contract officers. Every time

Lockheed forgets it and tries to sell an "industrial" product, the result is a disaster. Many suppliers of original equipment to the automobile manufacturers are in essentially the same strategic posture. There is ample history to demonstrate that it is a risky posture. If your channel pinches off for some reason, you seldom have many places to go.

Notice that this company says nothing about "manufacturing." This does not mean that it will not manufacture; remember, the mission statement is not proscriptive. It only says the company does not particularly expect to make its money on production. The company will keep its options open and manufacture when there is some advantage, but it could end up as a wholesale distributor and presumably be perfectly comfortable if that is the way to make the most money. Department store chains and supermarkets fall into this class, although they would probably use the word "merchandising" somewhere in their mission statement. Fast-food service chains, incidentally, do not. The successful ones are not selling-based or marketing-based but process-based. They succeed because they can serve food with a better price/quality relationship than anyone else. The chains that did not understand this went broke.

The Resource Managers

Our friends at XYZ might decide that their mission is:

> . . . to deploy the financial and other resources at our disposal so as to obtain the maximum return to our stockholders and the greatest opportunity for development for our employees.

In others words, they are going to be "resource managers." There is nothing inherently wrong in this despite the horrors that have been committed under such a banner. In some very large companies it is about the only way the top management can strategize, and even small, widely "diversified" companies may be able to find no other common strategic thread to hold the whole enterprise together. However, it is a scheme for specialists, for the rare "generalist" manager or for someone who has grown up in a successful "wheeler-dealer" organization.

Most managers who have grown up in one industry—be it food or any other—can't hack it. In the first place, they do not have the breadth of experience to enable them to make valid comparative evaluations of widely diverse opportunities. If they have production or marketing backgrounds, they have great difficulty remembering that success in the plant or in the market is no longer a prime consideration but that everything must now come down to plain old return on investment. If they come from finance, they usually do not have the operating experience required to hold a bunch of widely dissimilar operating units under control. Try it if you like, but be forewarned.

Try One On for Size

No matter which dimension you choose in defining your mission, remember it has two parts. It is not merely a matter of defining a market, although it must do that. It is not just deciding what you are best at, although you had better be good at what you decide to do. It should state what you are going to do for whom. If you do it right, it should position your company in such a function/market combination that it is easier for you to make money there than it is for anybody else. You want an "unfair" strategic advantage based on your unique circumstances. That's not illegal; that's just professional management.

For exercise, try writing a mission statement from each of the perspectives: raw materials, process, market, channel of distribution. You don't have to write the resource one because they are all alike. One of the alternatives may feel obviously comfortable, and you will know where you are at. If not, you have some heavy thinking to do and probably a lot of arguments in the process.

Divisional Missions

What if you are not in the top management of the company and do not have to grapple with "positioning" the company strategically? Do you still have to sweat out a mission statement for your area of responsibility? You certainly do. In some respects it is easier because you do not have to consider every conceivable alternative. Your position in the organization gives you some guidance and imposes certain constraints. However, it is unlikely to prefabricate your mission for you with sufficient definition to permit you to move into a strategic development with complete assurance.

If you are the head of an operating division or subsidiary, you do have the obligation to define the nature of the business you are pursuing, but usually with some limitations. Unless your organization is committed to a Darwinian style, pitting division against division in head-to-head competition for supremacy, you will have to avoid overlap with the roles assumed by other operating units.

Depending on the opportunities available to it, your corporate management also probably has some preconception of your division's proper place in the corporate scheme of things. Are you expected to be an aggressive salient on which much of the future growth of the company is dependent? Or are you the good reliable cash cow that provides the stability—and the cash flow—on which other more adventurous efforts can be based? Or something in between, or a mixture of both? Are you expected to exploit your resources worldwide, or is that somebody else's problem? May you move outside your existing product or market pattern, or are you expected to wring every last bit of benefit out of the fields you are in?

Getting the corporate brass to answer these questions may not be as easy as you would like. It's not fair, it's not smart, but it happens all the time. So hang in there and insist on a clear definition of just what your division's mission is. You will have a lot better chance of financial security in your old age if you do.

Very few corporate managements will "issue" a mission to a division. They seem to think that that would be dictatorial, or at least somehow "not nice." So you and your senior colleagues will have to start by trying to guess what the top management would like you to do. With that hypothesis in hand, you can try to combine it with what you think you ought to do or even just with what you would like to do. If the two pieces won't go together, you had better get it thrashed out now. If you are planting peaches and somebody else expects to harvest turnips, there is likely to be some noisy disappointment.

Departmental Missions

If you have a functional responsibility lower in the organization, you have the same kind of problem. Just what is your team supposed to accomplish over the long haul? Why is a sales department? Is it supposed to book maximum sales or generate maximum profit? To enhance share of market or to exploit access to a market to the greatest degree possible? Or just to keep the plant loaded? Or what? Unless you know, it is going to be pretty hard to make any long-range plans for the department.

If you have a staff department, the problem may have even fewer handles. Has anyone in your company ever really said why it maintains a public relations department? Or a personnel department? Or even an accounting department? Sure, the PR department certainly must do something useful and almost everybody has one, but just what is its reason for being? You may be surprised when you try to nail this down. So may some other people.

In a service department, maybe you can get by without a mission. Your superiors may not even think you need one. You should be around to do what you are asked to do. Well, all right. But you will be happier and will get a lot more satisfaction out of your work if you can get a clear understanding of just what your responsibilities are. And if you are going to make any long-range plans, you have to know what those responsibilities are.

You may find something like a mission statement at the top of your job description, but don't count on it. Job descriptions are seldom written from a strategic perspective.

What Does It Mean?

Now you have a mission statement written on that big blackboard. It supposedly says you are going to pursue a certain line of business to serve a certain delineated market. Stand back and see whether it *really* says anything—honestly. If the words are too loose, everyone is going to interpret them to suit his or her immediate purposes as time goes by, and you will not create the sense of common purpose you are striving for. Take it word by word and be sure that everyone at the meeting knows exactly what the words mean. Make an official thesaurus if you want. It won't hurt.

Do you talk about "quality products"? What do you mean by "quality"? Do you mean you are going to concentrate on the high-performance part of the line and stay out of the mass market? If that in fact is what you mean, can't you find some more meaningful way to state your intention? Or have you just put "quality" in there because it sounds good and strokes your ego? Do you say you are going to concentrate your marketing in the northeastern United States and "certain other markets"? What does "certain" mean? Does it mean any other market that somebody feels like investigating at a given point in time? If it does, you may as well scrap the whole phrase because it has no operational significance. If, on the other hand, it refers to specific isolated markets where you already have established dealerships, why don't you say so?

Do you talk about "widgets and related products"? Does everyone mean the same thing by "related"? If it means "accessories and supplies," fine—if everyone understands it that way. But it could mean "related" the way power boats are related to sailboats because they both float on the water. Do you refer to "retail food outlets"? Does that include McDonald's? It might, but if you mean grocery stores, then *say* grocery stores.

Be tough on yourself, even if you are doing the job solo. Be sure that the direction of the enterprise is as unambiguous as you can possibly make it. It will save immeasurable time and confusion in the future. There is a sort of Murphy's law of planning statements: "If anybody can misunderstand it, he will." Make it hard for them.

When you have your statement honed down just as fine as you can get it, get it typed up and have a copy put in front of everyone's planning book. Have it lettered on a flip sheet or show card and hang it on the wall every time you have a planning meeting. Do not have it cast in bronze yet, however, because you may find that you have to go back and modify it before you get through this planning cycle.

If this is a corporate mission statement and you have a board of directors that is more than a rubber stamp, take your draft mission statement to them and ask the members for their comments. Tell them that the mission cannot be finalized until you work through all the implications. What you want now is their general reaction. If any of them is strongly opposed and sees the business in a completely different light, you had better find out now before you do a lot more planning work. If there is a difference of opinion, it should be resolved now. Either you convince the board members, the board members convince each other, they convince you, or somebody resigns. They may say, "Work out the details and then we will decide." That is kind of a cop-out, but it leaves you no alternative but to "work out the details."

If this is not a corporate mission statement, then you have a boss; now is the time to negotiate with him or her just what your organizational unit is in business for. Before you agree to develop any long-range plans, insist that there be an agreement as to just what the mission of your operation is. If the boss waffles—and this might happen—at least you can put your mission statement on the front cover of any plans you submit, with an explicit declaration that this is the mission these plans are intended to fulfill. Presumably your boss will have to pass your plans up the line, at least for the record. If he or she won't, maybe your personal plans should include a change of venue.

SUGGESTED READING

Christopher, W. F., "Market Planning That Gets Things Done," *Harvard Business Review,* Vol. 48, No. 5 (September–October 1970).

Good discussion of definition of mission. Testifies that after ten years of zero sales growth and declining profits, Hooker Chemical Company introduced long-range planning. In the next five years, sales increased 14 percent per year and profits increased 21 percent per year.

Drucker, P. F., *The Practice of Management.* New York: Harper & Row, 1954. See especially p. 49.

One of Drucker's abiding themes has been the necessity to ask, "What is our business?" I believe that this is the first place he suggested in writing that failure to ask and adequately answer this question is the most important cause of business failure.

Levitt, T., "Marketing Myopia," *Harvard Business Review,* Vol. 38, No. 4 (July–August 1960).

Finally got the idea across that it is easier to sell what people want to buy. A classic.

3

You Must Have
Learned Something

Those who cannot remember the past
are condemned to repeat it.
G. SANTAYANA

PRESUMABLY you have been around your industry for some time. Hopefully you have learned something. You think you have some know-how, some business savvy. Okay, now is the time to put it on the line. If you expect to make every important decision for the company yourself over the next several years, you can do this job solo. It then becomes merely a matter of sitting down in a quiet place and writing down all the business principles that your experience has taught you are the wise ways to do things in your kind of endeavor. It is worth the effort. How many times have you ever said to yourself, "I knew better than to get into that kind of situation"? Maybe if you had written it down, you would have remembered that you knew better before you made the unwise commitment.

Most likely you have some responsible executives whose

judgment you do trust and whom you do expect to take independent action in matters of substantial importance to the company. Pick a day—possibly the day after your mission deliberations—make reservations at that hideaway away from the office, and get these people together. Conceivably this would be a different group, perhaps a larger group, than the one that worked with you on the mission decision. In the selection of the group your first criterion must be business judgment. Get the people who you think know the business and whose judgment you trust.

Presumably this group will include all or most of your immediate subordinates, but it might also comprise a board member or two, or an outside adviser. You may want to relax this fundamental criterion in a couple of special instances. If you have executives in the organization whom you want to make significant decisions and commitments for the company on occasion, it is important that they thoroughly understand the policy rationale of the organization. You might invite them to the meeting even if you do not expect them to provide much original input. However, do not go over a total of 12 members in your policy group. Eight or ten is a much better working maximum.

Tell your policy group in advance what you are trying to do—you are trying to crystallize the group's collective business wisdom and set it down in a set of ground rules to guide future strategic moves. This is not a matter of procedure or setting up a lot of niggling rules. It is not a job for clerks. It is an attempt to capitalize on the best business savvy that you have in your business organization.

The first thing to do when you get this group together is to tell them again that you are not there to discuss "policy" on maternity leaves, or what kind of items can be charged on an expense account, or even what to do with 30-day overdue receivables. The group will probably try to get off on such matters if you let them, and you will have to keep reminding them that this is a strategy session, not an operations meeting.

It is better not to start with a long list of functional areas in which you might establish policies, such as manufacturing, marketing, acquisitions, and credit. Sometimes this is the only way to get the deliberation going, but if you can stimulate the team to think about what they have learned about the general aspects of the business in some other way, you will come to the really critical issues quicker. With a laundry-list approach there is a compulsion to force the generation of some kind of policy on every subject. Such forced policy is often ill-conceived and sometimes completely impractical.

It Doesn't Have to Make Sense—It's Just Policy

There is a certain amount of validity in the sometimes snide comment, "It doesn't have to make sense—it's just policy." Where there is a clear-cut, rational approach to a business decision, you do not need policy. Policy comes into force only when you find yourself in the situation where you say, "It looks pretty good on the surface, but in the long run it's going to get us into trouble." In other words, policy bears on situations where your practical experience has told you that the odds are unfavorable even though in the specific case at hand it is hard to find justification for a decision one way or another. That is why policies can be justified only on the basis of judgment. There is no reason to apologize for this basis, nor is there any reason to fail to take advantage of this judgment by neglecting to set up a meaningful system of policy guidelines.

If you honestly feel that "we are after all a bunch of marketing people, and if we try to go into manufacturing we're going to get clobbered," then once and for all state as a policy that you are going to exploit your marketing capabilities and that you are not going to integrate backward into production unless the nature of the organization changes. If you feel that private-label manufacturing for potential competitors is cutting your own throat, then declare by policy that you will not do it except under certain specified, exceptional circumstances. If you feel that introducing "me too" products impairs the corporate image and never leads to a satisfactory profit situation, then say so. Even if the reason is only tradition and you cannot justify it any other way—"This company has never produced a product except from natural materials"—say so in your policy structure.

If you have strong ethical beliefs and you intend that they will influence the way the business is run, get them down in writing so there is no question about them. Don't kid yourself with, "We will be good citizens in all of the communities in which we operate." But if you intend ". . . to operate all facilities so that they fully comply with existing environmental control regulations at all times," say so—and be sure you mean it. It will establish priorities in the allocation of your resources.

The question is often raised, "Why write all these things down? We have a feel for the business, and we know how we do things and what we will do and won't do." Yes, you have a feel for the business, but the trouble is that feelings are notoriously individual. It is extraordinarily difficult to equate one person's "feel" with another's, no matter how closely they work together. As a practical fact, if you don't write down your policy structure, you end up with everyone making policy. The organization becomes infested with "We've never done it that way," or "I don't think *they* would let us do it," or "We tried that once and it didn't work." Unwritten policies can be much more restraining than a formalized policy structure.

See what kind of ground rules your policymakers can agree on. You may be surprised at the degree of disagreement. If there are disagreements that cannot be reconciled, the president has two choices. He can impose a policy either on a basis of majority decision or by simple personal fiat: "This is the way we are going to do things in the interests of consistency even if each of you individually does not agree that it is always the wisest course." Or he can simply say, "Since we can't agree on which is the wisest course in every case for this kind of decision, we will not establish policy on this matter and we will consider every situation as it comes up on a case-by-case basis."

Policies Are Time Savers

The second option suggests the real function of the policy structure. It is a time saver. It enables the management of the enterprise to proceed more quickly and with greater focus. It cuts down on meetings and memos. If you have to reinvent the wheel every time you get a flat tire, you will have a long, slow trip. But if you can agree in advance how you are going to respond to certain kinds of situations, you can get on with the job without so many conferences and consultations, and without wasting time on improbable sidetracks. It is true that policies by their very nature eliminate certain options, and some of those options conceivably could be potentially advantageous. However, if the judgment behind the policy decisions is sound, the odds are that the few winners you miss would not have provided enough benefits to counterbalance the trouble you would have gotten into if you had not had a policy guideline.

You may have as few as half a dozen strategic policies. It is improbable that the number would be more than 20 or 30 unless you let yourself slide into procedures and operational questions. If you can come up with only a handful of principles that you can codify into policy statements, there is a possibility that you really have not learned a great deal about the nature of your business. It may be that your peculiar business just does not have any consistent characteristics. However, it could be that you are really playing Russian roulette with the business and have never tried to generalize about the probabilities of what works out well and what is likely to be a bad business decision. You may just be a flabby management.

The extent of your fixed policy structure definitely reflects your management style. If you have a lot of policy, you can move quickly but down a fairly narrow track. If you have few set policies, you keep almost all your options open. But remember, keeping your options open can deteriorate into "riding off in all directions" or, worse, never making up your mind about what you ought to do.

Policies can be changed—you made them, you can change them—but if you do change policy, it should mean that you have learned something new or unlearned something that was wrong in the first place. Don't set policy with the mental reservation that you can always make exceptions. Yes, there can be exceptions to policy, but they should be made only under a fixed and formal procedure. Otherwise you're ". . . not that kind of a girl—unless someone asks me."

You will have individuals who won't take policies seriously—unless you make them. There's the person who is always slipping in the side door with a "special situation." Don't turn anyone off cold. Have him or her make a formal pitch before a policy group, recommending an exception to policy. The person may have something. Then again, maybe not, and after a few turndowns he or she will become much more thoughtful about such little adventures.

The same type may try a different tactic. He or she may object in principle to any policy structure at all because it would "stifle initiative" and make the organization "hidebound." The answer, of course, is that there is a vast difference between being "hidebound" and having a sense of direction and priority. No organization has such boundless resources that it can afford to entertain initiatives in all conceivable directions simultaneously. Your mission decision and your policy ground rules are intended to focus your attention on areas in which you have a maximum probability of success, given your particular circumstances. There should be plenty of room for fruitful initiative in and around the areas where you have special advantages.

You do have to avoid the rigid compulsive who wants a policy to cover every possible contingency. Such a course will make a lot of paperwork and may in fact get the place knotted up so it cannot move. As a practical matter, though, the more common consequence of too detailed a policy structure is a general loss of credibility as circumstances force more and more exceptions to policy.

When you agree on a set of strategic policies, get them typed and send a copy to each participant. The policy statements go right behind the mission statement in your planning book.

Take your policies to your board of directors. The board is nominally the policy-making group. However, you can tell the members that these are the strategic policies that you and your senior managers have agreed upon, and ask whether they would like to make any additions. Even an active board is unlikely to reverse your recommendations. Occasionally they may want to add to the policy structure. That is not only their privilege but their right.

It's not a bad idea to have recorded basic policies for an operating unit too, for the same reasons invoked for corporate policies. Of course these must be compatible with corporate policies and will be in addition to those policies. They should be developed and agreed upon by the leading managers of the operating unit on the basis of their collective judgment. Usually they will be submitted to the next higher level of management for approval, although this is not invariably required.

The Planning Horizon

There is one procedural matter that you should decide at this meeting: What is a reasonable planning horizon for your organization? There is nothing magic about a five-year planning period, although it is quite commonly used. The critical consideration is: How far out in time do you have to go to give yourself enough lead time to make really strategic changes in the direction of the enterprise? The minimum planning period is determined by how long it takes you to put new production facilities on stream, what your product development cycle is, how fast you can perfect new technology, how long it takes you to establish yourself in a new market, how fast you can open a new store. It is your knowledge of the natural cycles of your business—not some textbook—that determines what is the best planning period for you.

It would be a most chaotic business in which you could make meaningful strategic plans with a reach of less than three years. But three, four, five, six, ten years could be your particular minimum planning period. Start with the minimum realistic time horizon. As your planning gets more facile and sophisticated, you will probably want to extend the forward reach.

Most companies do. That is the time to do it—when it feels both comfortable and necessary.

There is a real correlation between the size of the organization being planned for and the time horizon of the plans. You can turn an outboard skiff around in its own length, but it takes miles to change the heading of a 100,000-ton tanker. Be realistic with yourself. If you are the head of a large operation, either a company or a division, there is almost nothing you can do to change strategic direction in a matter of months or maybe even years. The problem is compounded by the magnitude of the resources that must be redeployed, the cumulative resistance of individuals to change, and sheer organizational inertia. In fact, you can reverse this axiom and say that anything you can accomplish quickly probably is not very important anyway.

Empirically, you can observe a fairly regular relationship between the size of an organization and the time lag between executive decision and significant strategic impact. In a very small company the direction of thrust can be changed almost instantaneously. The time lag doubles with each order of magnitude in the size of the company; for a typical manufacturing/marketing company with $10 billion in sales, it is hard to effect really important changes in less than ten years. In a merchandising company, the lag is about half as long for any given sales volume, but for a professional service company like an engineering or accounting firm, the lag is doubled.

So pick a planning period that is at least as long as your turning radius. Otherwise all you will be doing is writing history. If you have no better basis, take your planning period from Figure 3 on the basis of your sales volume.

You don't have to have the same time horizon for all parts of your plan either. Facilities plans and sometimes financial plans may have to be made beyond the time scope of the corporate strategic plan. This leaves some uncertainty about the later years, but if it must be, it must be. Just because your plant is going to last for 10 or 15 years, don't waste a lot of time putting numbers in squares extending out through all those years if you can't honestly foresee market conditions or technological developments past the next five years.

Figure 3. Strategic time lag.

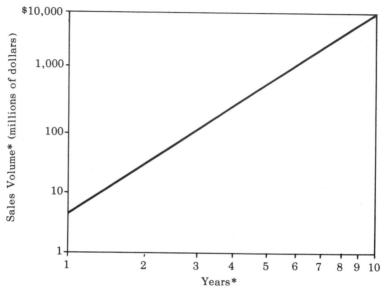

Logarithmic scale

Similarly, Figure 3 suggests that different parts of the organization might have different time horizons. It is quite common for a corporation to have a seven- or ten-year strategic plan and to ask its divisions, for, say, a five-year plan and its departments for a three-year plan. This scheme has the added advantage of keeping the boss a jump ahead of his subordinates —planningwise, at least.

SUGGESTED READING

Andrews, K., *The Concept of Corporate Strategy.* Homewood, Ill.: Dow-Jones-Irwin, Inc., 1971.

A good book, particularly the first two chapters on choosing directions and setting policies. However, Chapter 3 (on evaluating the company environment) and the last two chapters on organization and leadership are also good. Andrews approaches "strategy" as "the pattern of major objectives, purposes or goals and essential policies and plans for achieving those goals," as did Alfred Chandler in the classic Strategy and Structure. *So do I. Although I do not refer to "strategy" as such in this book, this is in no way intended to discount the importance of the concept commonly introduced under this term.*

Gray, E. (ed.), *Readings on Business Policy.* New York: Appleton-Century-Crofts, 1969.

This book actually relates policy formation so closely with corporate planning that fully one-third of the chapters are on corporate planning procedures.

Gross, A., and Gross, W. (eds.), *Business Policy: Selected Readings and Editorial Commentaries.* New York: The Ronald Press, 1967.

A collection of essays on the role of policy formation in corporate planning.

Koontz, H., and O'Donnell, C., *Principles of Management.* New York: McGraw-Hill Book Company, 1964, p. 87.

". . . a company should probably not plan for a longer period than is economically justifiable; yet it is risky to plan for a shorter period." Sounds reasonable, but not very helpful. As A. Lincoln said, "A man's legs should be long enough to reach from his body to the ground."

Newman, W. H., and Logan, J. P., *Business Policies and Central Management.* Cincinnati: South-Western Publishing Company, 1965.

Treats policy formation in the context of total corporate planning.

Salveson, M. E., "The Management of Strategy," *Long Range Planning,* Vol. 7, No. 1 (February 1974).

More on the natural time cycle of strategies, with some case histories.

Steiner, G. A., *Top Management Planning*. New York: The Macmillan Company, 1969, pp. 21–25.

Differentiates between the planning horizon and the length of the forecast period necessary for planning input. Reports several surveys and individual cases of planning and forecasting periods.

————, *Managerial Long-Range Planning*. New York: McGraw-Hill Book Company, 1963, pp. 44–48.

Reports an early seminar among planning experts who said about the same things then that they are saying now. Five years is a good planning period because four years seems too short and six years seems too long.

4
What's Going On in the World?

Results are obtained by exploiting opportunities, not by solving problems. All one can hope to get by solving a problem is to restore normalcy.
PETER DRUCKER

EVENTS that occur outside your organization will have more to do with its success than the initiatives you take unless you consciously turn the outside events to your advantage. In order to do that, you have to know what is going on. The more information you have about the business environment in which you have to function and the better you understand that information, the more likely you are to have a highly successful enterprise.

Market Analysis

The most important people in your external environment are your customers and your potential customers—your market. Who are they? What do they do? Why do they buy your product? What do they use it for? And most important, are there going to be more of them or fewer of them in the future? Are they going to buy more or less? Before you make any plans, find out the answers to these questions. If you can't find out the answers, guess. Your educated guesses are certainly better than nothing, and they may not be all that far off the mark. You cannot take concerted action at all without assuming something about your market. What are those assumptions? Why keep them a secret? Write them down so that you and everybody else knows the basis for your decision.

Tell your sales manager and marketing manager and product managers to get together and give you their best estimate of what the total market structure is and what it is likely to do throughout the planning period. Your sales manager and your marketing manager will be interested in a lot of details of the market analysis when they make their marketing plans, but for your corporate strategy purposes you are primarily interested in two factors: How fast is the market growing and who is supplying it?

You need to segment your market into groups of customer-product relationships that react in a more or less homogeneous manner—that is, where people are buying similar products for essentially the same reasons. Presumably these market segments will have distinctive development characteristics that will differ from group to group. Consequently you may have different strategies for each group. When very big companies segment their business this way, they talk about "business strategy areas."

You should not have more than ten such business segments or the paperwork will become overwhelming. You will have to lump some things together. But when you set up the categories, remember that you are trying to put together the things that will react in the market most nearly alike—not things that you make in the same plant or that use the same process or raw material. If some of the categories turn out to be too heterogeneous, someone may have to disaggregate them at a lower management level when you get some strategic planning going down there.

Any product group that provides less than 3 or 4 percent of your sales or profits—unless it is a new, fast developing business—does not warrant a separate strategy and should be dumped in "miscellaneous." If you have much over 10 percent of miscellaneous, though, you might begin to suspect that your company is a little unfocused. If you have one category that provides over 40 percent of your sales or profits, you might consider splitting it, not necessarily because the categorization is unsound but because you may be able to manage it better if you fine-tune the strategies a little more.

You will never have all the market information you want, so set yourself a deadline. Tell your market people that you want the best information and judgment they can muster within two months. And then tell them that a year from now you're going to ask for the same information again and that you will expect it to be better.

Actually, there is an amazing amount of market information available from government sources, trade sources, and the trade press. A whole profession of market researchers make a living sorting it out and rearranging it. Check your trade association. Contact the local field office of the U.S. Department of Commerce. That's what they're for—to guide you through the maze of government publications.

If you have your own market research people, fine. If you don't, consider buying market information. It is faster and possibly cheaper in the long run than trying to start from scratch yourself. There are all sorts of service organizations that would be delighted to accommodate you. The big houses and the research institutes will do highly detailed professional jobs and charge you as much as $100,000 or more. There are a lot of little quick-and-dirty shops very often specializing in a single industry; they will give you a good feel of the market dynamics for $5,000, $10,000, or $15,000.

The cheapest sources are undoubtedly the multiple-client market studies that have become popular in the past 20 years. There are a number of houses that specialize in these studies, which provide a broad survey of a certain market segment.

Some of the studies are sold "off the shelf," more or less

like expensive books. The better, and more expensive, ones are usually subscribed to in advance of the actual field work, but you can often get a copy "after the fact" at a premium price. Sometimes the cheaper studies are not too sophisticated, and in a few cases they are probably a little slapdash, but they are cheap. Many of them are sold in the range of $200 to $1,000. The more elaborate ones will go up to $15,000 or more per participation. There are very few consumer or industrial markets that have not been covered by such studies, and most of them have recycled every two or three years. The available studies will probably cover a broader market segment than you are interested in. That's how the service organizations insure a broad enough market so that they can make money. The statistical breakdowns may not be in just the form that you would prefer them. Well, you get what you pay for. The multi-client studies *will* give you an independent fix on the market, which at least you can check against your own estimates.

If there are no published market data for your business, then you will have to rely on guesses. But call it "judgmental forecasting." A few phone calls to knowledgeable people—the secretary of your trade association, a trade magazine editor, your suppliers, even your competitors—can sometimes be very informative. Even if they are guessing too, you can compare their guesses with yours.

If you want to do a field market study with your own people or commission it from a service firm, you can't do it in time for this planning cycle. Set it up now, though, so that you will have the results for next year.

You may have a little trouble with some of your sales people to get them to make a market forecast. They are apt to be used to making sales forecasts, short-range ones at that. You will just have to tell them that there is no one else in the company better qualified to predict what the market will do and that if they don't know, nobody does. If nobody in your organization knows what the dynamics of your market are, you are in trouble. Maybe you should put this book aside and start reading one on recruiting.

The professionals will tell you that you should not depend

on a sales force to make a market analysis; salesmen are too emotionally involved, don't often see beyond their immediate customers, and believe everything they want to believe. Furthermore, they are not really interested; they get paid for making sales, not for gathering information. This is probably all true, but if you don't have a market research staff and can't afford the time or money to contract outside for the study, your sales force is all you have. If necessary, bring in a pro to give them a one-day short course in market analysis. Your sales managers ought to know something about market research anyhow. You will have to depend on them to guard you against inspired fiction made up at the last minute because the field man didn't take the time to get any real data.

What you want most out of your market analysis is trend. A snapshot—that is, a breakdown of the market for any one year—is of relatively little use for strategy purposes. You need some history. Get as many years as you can without expending an exorbitant effort. People say that you can't plan in a rear-view mirror, but the somewhat disconcerting fact is that there is a kind of Newton's law of market movement. A market trend tends to stay in motion along a constant line unless acted upon by some extraordinary new event in the environment. Thus in hindsight, some rather simple-minded statistical extrapolations have proved to be as accurate as other much more sophisticated market-forecasting techniques, at least for relatively short periods like five to ten years.

So ask your marketing people to pick off the trends that seem to have been operating in the past. If you have some curve-fitting routines on your computer, fine; use them. Otherwise the average annual percentage growth is easy to calculate and it ain't bad. It will give you a kind of baseline on which to apply your perceptions of the future market environment. If your marketing people have reason to believe that the trends won't hold, ask for their forecast and the reasons for the difference from the extrapolation.

I suggest that you record your market numbers in current dollars—that is, the kind of dollar that appears on your periodic operating statements—so that you don't have to get involved with price deflaters every time you compare actual performance with plan. This means that you have to find out how much of the growth is real and how much of it is only price inflation.

If you are dealing with a product in which you have good volume numbers, it is very easy to compare growth of physical volume with growth in dollar sales and see how much of the dollar number is price inflation. If this cannot be easily done, your first step is to go back over your price history and see how much price escalation you have introduced over the past five or ten years. Since you were presumably price-competitive during that historical period, your price actions have to have been fairly characteristic of the industry. Ultimately you want two curves: one for dollar growth and one for growth in physical volume or some comparable consumption figure.

Competitive Analysis

While sales and marketing are documenting the dynamics of the market, you can start working on the other thing you want to know about your market: Who is serving it and how well? Sit down with your sales manager and list the top six suppliers to each market segment. Hopefully this list will include yourself. Now try to put some percentage share of market alongside each supplier in that list and rank it from high to low. You don't need tremendous accuracy. Plus or minus a couple of percentage points is almost always good enough.

We may not always like to admit it, but the FTC boys have a point when they complain about "concentration" in an industry. Has one supplier as much as 40 percent of the market? Have three got as much as 60 percent of the market together? Do four have 75 percent of the market? If so, look out. This is going to be a tough business in which to make a buck, unless of course you are one of the concentrators. If you are fourth or fifth or seventh or eighth in a "concentrated" market, you had better have something very special going for you if you expect to make any kind of impressive strategic record.

Unless you have special product technology, or a particular cost advantage, or a big chunk of captive market, or some other extraordinary circumstance, you had better try to find a more promising way to make money. Narrow your target market so you are not slugging it out with the big companies. Take the same product out into a completely new market. Can you sell your Caribbean cruises to gay groups, for instance? There are a few successful Davids in the business wars, but most of them end up with their heads split open.

Now get in your production team—your chief purchasing agent, your chief of manufacturing, your chief engineer. Ask them to rank your competitors in terms of manufacturing costs. You may be surprised to find out how much they know about other people's plant costs. They know their labor rates. They know what they are paying for raw materials. They know how big their plants are and what kinds of processes they use. If they don't, they should.

Ask the engineer to stick around, and call in your director of research—if you have one—and your product managers, if you have any. Ask them to rank your competitors according to the technical quality of their product or service.

If it is significant in your business, ask the marketing and sales people to rank the competition on distribution system and customer service. Then, finally, you and your financial officer rank competitors in terms of financial resources. How deep a pocket do they really have if they want to launch a new line, install a new technology, or go into a price war?

You could do all this with a memorandum questionnaire, but you will learn something from the justification of the ranking that you get in a face-to-face discussion and possibly from disagreements among the various people present. If you have a small organization, you can get the whole team together at one session and consider these various dimensions all at once.

What kind of pattern do you see? Given a reasonable amount of self-flattery, you ought to have at least one first-place ranking for your own company, possibly two, and a couple of twos or threes in each product category. If you do not, you have put yourself in a rough game. You are going to be playing catch-up all the time unless you can find some special niche for yourself that gives some promise of persisting over a reasonable period of time. You could find that niche by segmenting the market.

Pick a part of the market—defined by geography, price, customer group, technology, or whatever—and concentrate on becoming a dominant factor in that submarket rather than trying to cover the whole line. If you cannot devise such a unique strategy, you had better make plans to withdraw from that product line and perhaps go back and rewrite that mission statement.

Analysis of General Environment

The market and the competition is the easy part of the environment to understand. It is the part that you live most closely with, that you have the most contact with, that you pay most attention to. Unfortunately the developments in the environment that are most likely to have major impact on your future business may arise outside your immediate business circle. Laws get passed or reinterpreted. New technologies arise out of completely unrelated industries. People change their buying or living habits. Foreign trade patterns change. Neighborhoods change. Raw material supplies dry up or become oppressively expensive. These kinds of changes usually do not occur quickly; but unfortunately when they become easily apparent, it is frequently too late to do anything about them. Constructive responses require long lead times and have to be started well in advance of the critical phase of the change.

Spotting major environmental developments takes a certain amount of vision. It definitely requires getting out of the trees of current operations to take a look at the shape of the forest. Go back to that retreat again with the same team you had for your policy meetings. You may want to add the head of market research or additional technical people of the type who are particularly comfortable dealing with events in the future. Take a half day, a whole day if you can swing it. Try to get one of the professional futurists to give you a one-hour presentation to begin your sessions. He probably will not tell you much that you can use directly, but the idea is to open up minds and break down the habitual patterns of thought. You will want a lot of blackboard space or a couple of flip-sheet pads on easels. Start writing down a list of things that are happening, or might happen, outside the company and which could have a major impact on the nature of your business—its profitability, its sales volume, or maybe its survival. Get everybody into the act. Consider legal developments, political developments, international developments, technology, social patterns, demography, consumer habits, distribution patterns, industry organization.

If you are like most managements, you will end up with one helluva laundry list. Now analyze these items, using three categories: Could they possibly (1) increase or decrease your sales or your earnings by 10 percent in the next full fiscal year, or (2) increase or decrease your sales or your earnings by 50 percent in five years, or (3) put you out of a major part of your business or triple the business potential within ten years? Be honest, but not alarmist. The items that do not fall into any of these classes are interesting, but so what? Forget them, at least until next year. This should shorten the list considerably, and you can put it on a tally sheet such as that in Figure 4.

The items in category one obviously need the most immediate attention. What do you think the odds are that the development will actually occur and impact your business? One in ten? You had better keep an eye on the situation, but you can't afford to respond to such long odds. One in three? Assign someone to look into the situation, get more information, and confirm your estimate of the probabilities.

If your first guess proves to be about right, have somebody look into it further and sketch out a contingency plan in three or four pages. If the impact on you will be negative, what can you do to cut your losses or eliminate your exposure to losses altogether? If the impact is positive, how can you position your affairs so as to take maximum advantage of the opportunity should it arise? If you approve the general outlines of the

Figure 4. Environmental analysis — 1975.

Environmental Event	EXPOSURE			Earliest Possible Year	PROBABILITY						Company Response Time, Yrs.	Watch	Investigate	Contingency Plan	Action Plan
	10% Next Year	50% in 5 Years	100% in 10 Years		10%	30%	50%	70%	90%	50/50 year					
A	+				X							J. Doe			
B	–					X							M. Roe	?	
C	+							X							Smith
D		–		1977						1978	1	L. Brown			
E		–		1976						1978	2		K. Jones	?	
F		+		1977						1977	3				Douglas
G			+	1977						1979	4				Curtis
H			–	1978						1980	3			L. Lewis	

+ = opportunity   – = threat

contingency plan, tell the person who made it to keep an eye on the situation and report to you when and if he or she thinks it is appropriate to consider putting the plan into action.

If you think the odds are two out of three that the environmental development you have identified is going to happen within the next several months, you had better assume that it *will* happen, and act as if you were certain of the event. Get somebody on the job and start taking steps either to reduce your exposure or to increase your capability to respond to the opportunity. This will cost a little money and it could be wasted, but if 10 percent of your business is at stake, the gamble is pretty good at two-to-one odds.

I know these are supposed to be long-range strategic planning sessions and that next year's developments are not exactly long range. They are practically tomorrow. However, there is no reason to be academic about any of this. If you identify a short-range operational planning problem, do something about it now. Then you can get back to the strategy sessions.

In other categories where long time periods are involved, the first thing you want to do is find out the minimum time you have to react. Put your heads together and decide what is the *earliest possible time* at which such a development could have a noticeable effect on your business. If it is a new process, how long will it take for it to be perfected, built, installed, in production? If it is a law, what is the soonest it could get through the legislature and be in force? If it is a consumer attitude, how fast do you think people can change to the extent that it begins to be reflected in your sales reports?

Now, what is your response time? How long does it take you to develop and introduce a new process, to reformulate your product, to modify your marketing approach? If your response time is less than the time to the earliest possible impact date for the change, put the item on the agenda for the planning sessions next year and let it lie for the present. In other words, if you feel that it would be impossible for new legislation to get through the legislature before next year and that it could not be put into force until the following year, and if you are confident that you can reformulate, test, and get approval of a modified product in 12 months, you have a year's grace and do not need to make a decision about it until next year.

Now your list is shorter yet. On those remaining items, what is your judgment of the 50/50 year—the year by which you think the event is just as likely to occur as not? For the items in category two, the 50 percent impact ones, if the 50/50 year is beyond the lead time you require to make a constructive response, have somebody look into the situation to check your evaluation of the probabilities; then you can probably gamble for another year before you take any action. If the 50/50 year is already within your effective response lead time, you had better start doing something about it. You cannot afford to ignore a threat of this magnitude to your company, nor should you pass up an opportunity with these possibilities. Set up a project, with a good man in charge of it, and see what he can come up with as an action plan in this situation.

The category three items have the potential to cripple your company seriously or, alternatively, to put it into a major growth phase. Since your estimate of the earliest possible date is already within your effective response lead time, you must begin an action plan immediately. If the 50/50 date is beyond your estimated lead-time requirement, your project may be designed somewhat more tentatively than the category two items that were mentioned above, but you must make an active beginning because your response could be delayed until some time after the need became apparent. If the 50/50 estimated date is at or within your lead time, you will want to set up an action project on a crash basis. You have to assume that the forecast date is accurate because the consequences are too critical if you miss the deadline.

In all cases, of course, you will reevaluate your time line as you do your annual recycle of plans, and will accelerate or stretch out your programs as your perceptions of the probability of change are modified.

What you have just done is sometimes called a "threats and opportunities" analysis. There are many more elaborate techniques for environmental analysis, including the whole spectrum of devices called technological forecasting, technology assessment, and futurology generally. If you want to look into them, see the suggested readings, but realize that they are time-consuming and expensive, and can be confusing if your overall planning system is relatively unsophisticated.

SUGGESTED READING

Ansoff, H. I., *Corporate Strategy*. New York: McGraw-Hill Book Company, 1965.

Still a good basic approach to forming strategy in response to external events. A little complicated and academic in spots, but based on much perceptive observation. Some good checklists. Good on diversification. A most welcome emphasis on profitability.

Aguilar, F. J., *Scanning the Business Environment*. New York: The Macmillan Company, 1967.

A good basic treatment.

Denning, B. W., "Strategic Environmental Appraisal," *Long-Range Planning*, Vol. 6, No. 1 (March 1973), pp. 22–27.

A scheme for gathering and appraising environmental information in terms of impact on a single company.

Ferrell, R. W., *Customer-Oriented Planning*. (AMACOM, 1968), chap. 1–6.

A somewhat different planning sequence, but good solid stuff on responding to the environment.

Forster, N. F., *Published data on European Industrial Markets*. London: Industrial Aids, Ltd., 1975.

A cross-indexed annotated list of multiple client studies, but it is not complete for the United States. Charles Klein, Inc., 369 Pas-

saic Avenue, Fairfield, New Jersey 07006, will have one out for this country early in 1976.

Kahn, H., and Bruce-Biggs, B., *Things to Come—Thinking About the 70's and 80's.* New York: The Macmillan Company, 1972.

A mind-stretcher.

Kastens, M. L., "Outside-In Planning," *Managerial Planning,* Vol. 22, No. 5 (March–April 1974).

More on taking advantage of external events.

Linstone, H., and Turoff, M., *The Delphi Method and Its Application.* New York: American Elsevier Publishing Company, 1973.

A detailed discussion of one way of processing expert opinions about the future, which has gotten a lot of publicity.

Martino, J., *Technological Forecasting for Decision Making.* New York: American Elsevier Publishing Company, 1972.

An overview of forecasting techniques and approaches to disciplined speculation. Not limited to technological probabilities.

Merrill, T. P., "Forecasting the Business Environment—The State of the Art," *Long-Range Planning,* Vol. 7, No. 2 (June 1974).

Review of forecasting techniques. Sources of market data in Europe.

U.S. Department of Commerce, *Industry Profiles.* Washington, D.C.: U.S. Government Printing Office, 1971.

Gives gross margins, inventories, wage rates, and so on for industry groups by four-digit SIC code.

5

Meanwhile,
Back at the Shop

If we could know where we are and whither we are tending, we could then better judge what to do and know how to do it.
ABRAHAM LINCOLN

THE analysis of the internal characteristics of an organization is a very highly developed art and skill. There is an extensive literature on the subject, some of which is extremely sophisticated and mathematically complex. For the purposes of this planning cycle, we will use a very much simplified technique to identify the extreme characteristics of the enterprise with which we would want to deal directly in our strategic plans. Take the charts given in Figure 5, modify and enlarge them as you think appropriate to your particular organization, and distribute them to your policy group. Ask these people to rank your organization by checking the columns as indicated.

Weaknesses

Set up a one-day meeting and ask your colleagues to bring their rating sheets with them. When the group has assembled,

Figure 5. Operational evaluation.

Check off in each category how you evaluate your organization according to:

Column I	Better than anyone else. Substantially in excess of present needs. Definitely leaders.
Column II	Better than average. Good strong performance. No problems.
Column III	Average. Adequate. Competitive. Solid.
Column IV	Should be better. Deteriorating. Cause for concern.
Column V	Definitely worrisome. Must be improved. Bad. Crisis. "We are being clobbered."

Category	I	II	III	IV	V
Finance					
Debit-equity structure	___	___	___	___	___
Inventory turnover	___	___	___	___	___
Customer credit	___	___	___	___	___
Capital resources	___	___	___	___	___
Available cash flow	___	___	___	___	___
Break-even points	___	___	___	___	___
Sales per assets employed	___	___	___	___	___
Ratio fixed to liquid assets	___	___	___	___	___
Performance versus budget	___	___	___	___	___
Return on new investments	___	___	___	___	___
Ownership	___	___	___	___	___
Dividend history	___	___	___	___	___
Production					
Capacity	___	___	___	___	___
Production processes	___	___	___	___	___
Conversion efficiency	___	___	___	___	___
Labor supply	___	___	___	___	___
Labor productivity	___	___	___	___	___
Raw material supply	___	___	___	___	___
Sales per employee	___	___	___	___	___
Sales per fixed investment	___	___	___	___	___
Age of plant equipment	___	___	___	___	___
Quality control	___	___	___	___	___
On-time shipments	___	___	___	___	___
Downtime	___	___	___	___	___
Space for expansion	___	___	___	___	___
Plant location	___	___	___	___	___

Figure 5. (continued)

Category	I	II	III	IV	V
Organization and Administration					
Ratio of administrative to production personnel	___	___	___	___	___
Communications	___	___	___	___	___
Clear-cut responsibilities	___	___	___	___	___
Management turnover	___	___	___	___	___
Management information	___	___	___	___	___
Speed of reaction	___	___	___	___	___
Marketing					
Share of market	___	___	___	___	___
Product reputation	___	___	___	___	___
Brand acceptance	___	___	___	___	___
Selling expense	___	___	___	___	___
Customer service	___	___	___	___	___
Distribution facilities	___	___	___	___	___
Sales organization	___	___	___	___	___
Prices	___	___	___	___	___
Number of customers	___	___	___	___	___
Distribution costs	___	___	___	___	___
Market information	___	___	___	___	___
Manpower					
Hourly labor	___	___	___	___	___
Clerical labor	___	___	___	___	___
Sales people	___	___	___	___	___
Scientists and engineers	___	___	___	___	___
Supervisors	___	___	___	___	___
Middle management	___	___	___	___	___
Top management	___	___	___	___	___
Training costs	___	___	___	___	___
Management depth	___	___	___	___	___
Turnover	___	___	___	___	___
Technology					
Product technology	___	___	___	___	___
New products	___	___	___	___	___
Patent position	___	___	___	___	___
R&D organization	___	___	___	___	___
Engineering design capability	___	___	___	___	___

start looking down the sheets for items checked in column V.
When anyone has one, have him or her defend the evaluation
until the group agrees that this aspect of the operation either
is in fact a potential catastrophe or is merely a problem that
should be classified in column IV.

When you have completed checking the lists, you will have
identified what are usually called your "corporate weaknesses."
It is important that you do this job very objectively. You don't
want to be stampeded by the Cassandras who are sure everything is going to go to hell tomorrow morning. You are looking for problem areas that presently prevent you from getting
up any strategic momentum or for situations in which you are
so vulnerable that a unilateral action by a competitor (or by
your bank) could pull the rug out from under you. Be sure
you spot them if they are there. If you try to paper over a true
strategic weakness, your plans will never eventuate because
the organization's vitality will be sapped in trying to compensate for it.

If you do not have any entries under column V, you are
either lucky or dangerously complacent. If you do have entries
in column V, you should not have more than two or three of
them unless you are a very sick company or are a bunch of
nervous nellies.

In any case, to the extent that you have strategic weaknesses, you will have to take another detour from your long-
range planning in order to insure that the company does in
fact have a future. If your assessment of these operational
characteristics is valid, then no long-range plan is going to
work unless you can shore up these areas. There is no point in
waiting until you have completed your long-range plan before you start doing something about these problems because
you know already that they will have top priority for your resources. You may as well get something started now. If it takes
the rest of the day, you will have to schedule another session
to complete the operational analysis.

The first thing you need to do is to set up an objective to
eliminate the weakness. Remember, you do not want to get
your resources all tied up in trying to make every aspect of the

operations perfect. All you want is to move the situation from column V to column IV so that you can get on to doing something more creative. What would be the circumstances under which you would move this situation over to column IV—not to bring it to the point where you wouldn't try to improve it, but just good enough so that it no longer would prevent you from fulfilling your more aggressive strategies? Define those circumstances, and that's your objective.

Your objective could be to walk away from the weakness. Weaknesses are not absolute. They are only relative to what you are trying to do. Weighing 140 pounds could be a tremendous disadvantage if you tried to play big-time football, but it might be great if you wanted to be a middle-distance runner. If you are underfinanced, maybe you'd be better off to get out of the product line with the long receivables rather than try to recapitalize. If your production costs are inherently high, don't try to compete in the long-production-run, price-sensitive markets. Go after the markets where your production flexibility is valuable and price is not so important.

You will want to set up a project to correct each one of these weaknesses and to put a project leader in whom you have complete confidence in charge of each one. If he or she has to be relieved of continuing responsibilities to do it, these duties will have to be at least temporarily delegated to some less competent person. It always takes less competence to continue to administer an ongoing function than to create an innovative approach to a specific problem. Correcting these weaknesses is going to require an innovative approach because they obviously have arisen as a result of the way you have been doing things in the past. Doing these same things *harder* is not going to correct the problem and in fact may accentuate it. Therefore, it is unlikely that the person currently responsible for the function in which the weakness arises will be the best one to head the project to correct it. If he or she recognized the problem and knew how to correct it, but didn't, he or she ought to be fired anyhow.

It is quite possible that some of the weaknesses you have identified arise from an environmental threat that you dis-

cussed at your last session. If you have already assigned someone to propose an action plan to meet that threat, that plan
will now be absorbed in the program to eliminate the weakness. You may want to retain the same leader or to beef up the
effort because the conjunction of a threatening external environment with an organizational deficiency is a particularly
hazardous condition.

If the person you decide to put in charge of correcting the
weakness is not at the meeting, try to get him or her to join the
meeting immediately so that you can collectively review the
reasons why you all agreed that this situation had to be cor-
rected before you could hope to move the enterprise toward
any new ground. You want to consciously create in that person
and in your own group a sense of urgency. It is amazing how
many strategic weaknesses persist for years after they have
been identified as substantial barriers to any significant progress in the company. And then the management wonders why
it is not keeping up with its long-term objectives.

The trouble is that strategic weaknesses are not like an
operational crisis. They are not noisy or exciting, unless the
competition moves strongly to exploit them, and then it is too
late. No! Strategic weaknesses bog things down; they gnaw;
they enervate; but they don't *demand* attention. Furthermore,
they are unpleasant to think about and often difficult and perhaps embarrassing to correct.

So once you have one on the hook, don't let it get away—
even overnight. Decide *now* who is going to be responsible
for correcting it, although not necessarily how he or she will
go about it. Get the person into conference as fast as possible,
explain the problem as well as you know how, and state the
objective. Ask the person how soon he or she can be back to
you with a proposed course of action along with cost and time
estimates. Set up a meeting to hear the proposal and approve
implementation. Particularly, tell the person how his or her
regular work is going to get done while he or she is on this
special assignment. If you expect this manager to correct strategic weaknesses in his or her spare time, forget it. Anyone
who has that much spare time is not the right person for the
job.

If the manager is good enough to do the job, he or she may not be overjoyed with the assignment because cleaning up messes is not the most glamorous kind of work, and he or she also may have to step on some toes. The only thing you can do is impress on the manager the importance of the job—that really all the exciting things the company wants to do have got to be sidetracked until this thing is cleared up. Then tell the person that you are just as eager as he or she is to get him or her off the job. The sooner the objectives can be achieved, the better you will like it, and you will be delighted to put the responsibility back into the regular administrative structure at the earliest possible moment.

Strengths

Now let's get back to the operational analysis rating sheets (Figure 5). Go down column I until you can all agree on just which items ought to be checked in that category. These are strategic strengths, and you ought to be able to figure out a way to do something with them—to make an extra buck out of them. They are in effect idle resources that are lying around in the back lot and should be exploited. It will inevitably be easier to build new strategies on these existing strengths rather than to start something up with no particular advantage, no matter how attractive the potential might be. First use up what you have before you go out and buy new resources.

However, when you try to find a way to exploit these strengths, you may find that there is still quite a bit of simple self-congratulation in the list. If you really do something "better than anyone else," it is almost certain that someone will pay for it. If they won't, the item probably belongs in column II.

Of course you may also find that you do not have excess resources to exploit, that each resource is good but not "substantially in excess of present needs." You may have beyond question the greatest field sales force in the business, but they may be running their legs off. There is no way you can capitalize on this "strength" by distributing additional products through the organization. If you took on additional products, you would have to hire more salespeople. So even if your performance is superior, but there is no slack left to work with, this "strength" has to be downgraded to column II.

Don't flatter yourself that just because you are proud of the way you do something, anybody else really cares. On the other hand, don't give up too easily. A lot of companies, of all sizes, have developed profitable sidelines selling their staff services outside the company—sometimes even to competitors. Engineering design and construction, instrumentation, market research, industrial engineering, management development, and planning and product introduction capabilities have all been exploited in this way.

Patent licensing is an obvious possibility. Excess capacity may be salable for toll processing or custom packing. A well-established brand may be spread over additional, possibly unrelated, products—although that's a tricky one and has probably failed more often than it has succeeded. A fat balance sheet may permit favorable acquisitions or rapid expansion. An exceptional research capability can be extended into completely new applications. A production technique that you developed for one purpose may have all sorts of unrelated applications. Even skills in physical distribution have been capitalized on strategically.

The trick in strategizing strengths is usually to be able to view them as though you were outside the organization. If you have unexploited capability that could be utilized more extensively or intensively within the existing operations of the company, it would seem to imply negligence on somebody's part. It is quite likely that the market that would "buy" your exceptional capability will use it for something different than you do. That means you have to "generalize" your strengths and understand their essential character, not just see them in the function where they are of value to you. It is not that you can make glass fibers but that you can handle high-temperature extrusions. It is not that you can sell filter cloth but that you have good acceptance among the people who buy filter media. It is not that you can deliver a quality product but that you have quality control systems and instrumentation that nobody else has.

Several years ago, Du Pont realized that it had a large and highly competent instrument engineering group, developed to meet its own requirements. But the instrument industry was highly profitable and growing very rapidly. Now Du Pont has an instrument division that is expanding aggressively. More recently the company established a public consulting service.

Home delivery of milk is falling off rapidly in the United States. There are complications in delivering anything but milk in a milk truck, *but* dairies do have a great deal of skill in routing and scheduling home-delivery systems. They have found a number of markets for that skill and recently began to take over the delivery of mass circulation periodicals from the U.S. Postal Service.

Probably the most spectacular example of the strategic exploitation of a basic strength has been in the evolution of the 3M Company. Virtually its entire early development and much of its subsequent growth has been attributable to finding new uses for a single, highly developed production technique. The company went from sandpaper to roofing materials to Scotch tape to magnetic tape to photocopying to reflective signs. These are widely different markets, different kinds of applications, different competitive conditions. But all these products are based upon the ability to lay down a closely controlled layer of material on a flexible substrate. The 3M Company is still looking for new places to cash in on this exceptional know-how.

Going further back in time, when Du Pont consciously reoriented itself from a powder company to a manufacturer of chemicals, it chose its strategy on the basis of what it knew how to do better: conduct chemical reactions on an industrial scale. The result is very impressive history.

What capabilities do you have that might be extended to new applications or generalized to serve other people's needs? Has your past necessity mothered inventions that can solve other people's problems as well as yours? You will never know unless you think about those other people's problems.

There is no reason to feel embarrassed if you identify only one or two or no "strengths" in this exercise because we are using a very special and limited definition of the term. We are looking specifically for a resource that has potential for strategic exploitation. If there were too many such resources lying around idle, it might imply a rather slack management. Contrariwise, if there are no available "strategic strengths," it could mean that you are using all your resources right up to the hilt—but don't count on it.

If you did look at your capabilities from the "outside-in," it is quite likely that the exploitability of one of your strengths arises out of an opportunity situation that you have identified in the outside world. In that case you can combine your "opportunity" and your "strength" projects. One warning: Be sure you did not "invent" the strength because you were so eager to take advantage of the opportunity. Don't kid yourself!

The interaction between a "threats and opportunities" analysis and a "strengths and weaknesses" analysis is to be expected because strategic strengths and weaknesses only exist relative to the demands that you or the environment will make on the organization. That is why you have to do the environmental analysis first—to provide a framework against which to evaluate the capabilities of the organization. Like the fellow said: "How's your wife?" Reply: "Compared to what?"

If you have made several action plan assignments for threats and opportunities and a couple for weaknesses, you quite possibly are beginning to run out of good people. You will have to start setting priorities. Without question the first call has to go to programs to eliminate weaknesses. If you don't get these situations shored up, nothing else is going to work because that is how you *defined* a weakness.

The person you put in charge of a weakness project is already working on his or her action plan and will put it into operation as soon as it is approved. If that manager has committed himself or herself to achieving his or her objectives early next year, you can plan the person into a more adventurous assignment at that time.

If your analysis has been sound, ventures based on strategic strengths should have the highest probability of success and the earliest payback. They should get next priority. Have you got good people to put on them? If you have a venture management group, of course you already have people identified and organizationally designated for this purpose. More likely you will have to take somebody out of an ongoing assignment.

If you don't have a first-rate venture manager to assign, hold the project until you do. There is no point in putting a second-rate manager in charge of a venture project. He or she will have neither the judgment nor the imagination to exploit the opportunity properly and will either muff it because of overconservatism or get you into trouble by going off half-cocked. Wait until someone who can do the job right is available.

If you can assign a venture manager at this time, ask the person to develop an action plan proposal that is to be implemented starting next year but that is to be presented for review and tentative approval in two months.

The assignments already made to propose action plans to respond to threats and opportunities that have not been rolled up in strength and weakness assignments should be allowed to proceed to completion. The proposals are due in a couple of weeks anyhow. If at that time the decision should be made to shelve any of those projects, a manager might be available for reassignment to a suspended strength-exploiting venture.

SUGGESTED READING

Anonymous, "GE's New Strategy for Faster Growth," *Business Week* (July 8, 1972).

How GE segments its business into "strategic business units."

Beyer, R., *Profitability Accounting for Planning and Control.* New York: The Ronald Press, 1963.

Standard review of management information and control systems. There are undoubtedly others just as good.

Branch, M. C., *The Corporate Planning Process*. (AMACOM, 1962).

Chapter V, pp. 121–180, by E. C. Nelson and M. C. Branch, titled "Techniques of Analysis," is a good review of the theoretical state of the art at that time. The practices of most companies have not yet caught up to that level of sophistication.

DeCoster, D. T., Rainanathan, K. V., and Sundem, G. L., *Accounting for Managerial Decision Making*. Los Angeles: Melville Publishing, 1974.

A smorgasbord of readings by various authors from a spread of disciplines concerned with the analysis and use of operating data. A good sampling.

Ferguson, C. R., *Measuring Corporate Strategy*. Homewood, Ill.: Dow-Jones-Irwin, 1974.

Introduces a technique called the "concept audit" to determine just what an organization thinks it's doing. Not the usual operational analysis, but an interesting idea.

Levin, R. I., and Kirkpatrick, C. W., *Quantitative Approaches to Management*. New York: McGraw-Hill Book Company, 1965.

One of several similar books that try to introduce practicing managers to the newer analytical techniques. None of them relates as clearly to the real world as you would wish.

Salveson, M. E., "Strategy of Innovation in Technical Industries" in *Long-Range Planning*, Ewing, D. (ed.). New York: Harper & Row, 1968.

Strategizing from technological strengths.

6
Where Do You Want to Go?

"Would you tell me, please, which way I ought to go from here?"
said Alice.
"That depends a good deal on where you want to get to,"
said the Cat.
"I don't much care where . . . ," said Alice.
"Then it doesn't matter which way you go," said the Cat.
LEWIS CARROLL

THE essential characteristic of "planned management" as opposed to crisis management is that it works from ends to means, from results to actions. Crisis management says: "Well, we got so and so done yesterday. What should we do today?" Planned management asks: "If we want to accomplish so and so, what can we do immediately to start moving in that direction?" It does not take the amateur inventor's approach of: "I wonder what would happen if we tried such and such an experiment." Rather, like the professional scientist, it says: "According to the best information I can assemble, this procedure should lead to a certain predetermined result. Now let's try it out and see if the hypothesis is sound." Neither approach can absolutely guarantee success, but in both science and management the planned approach has proved to be a great deal more efficient.

You have decided what kind of business you want to be in. You have set some ground rules for your strategic decisions. You have tried your best to understand the external environment within which you have to operate. You have looked at yourself with as much objectivity as you can muster and have inventoried your resources. Your market analysis should now be available. Given that situation, what do you think you should reasonably be expected to accomplish?

No single indicator by itself will give a clear-cut reading of the success of a business. You want profit. You want growth. You want reasonable protection from exposure to excessive risk. You want long-term stability. Not only do these various objectives have to be measured in different terms, but they tend to be mutually antagonistic. Growth is achieved at the expense of profit. Current profits may be realized at the expense of long-term position in the market. Both growth and profit can be obtained only by accepting certain risks. Stability moderates growth. You need a set of primary objectives that will give you a multidimensional indication of how successfully you are managing your business.

The way you balance off the various primary objectives is a highly judgmental matter. It says a great deal about your individual and corporate personality and about your fundamental business judgment.

Because primary objectives are subjective and judgmental, you must have absolute commitment to them by the key people who are going to make them happen. To get the kind of commitment you need, these people not only have to understand the nature and implications of the objectives; they have to be party to setting them. Get together all the people who report directly to you. Go out to your hideaway. Figure on at least a long day for the first session.

When you get this group together, tell them that you are going to try to agree on the definition of successful management of your business. Since you fully intend to be successful, once you have this agreement you expect everyone to accept these objectives as a commitment to performance. These are not pious hopes or "wouldn't it be nice if" dreams; they are management's performance specifications. If they are not achieved, someone has failed, and therefore top management has failed.

If these specifications are to be of any use, they must be specific. This means in almost all cases that they will be quantitative or at least quantifiable. It means more than that; in addition to being numerical, the language around the numbers must be as unambiguous as you can possibly make it. Leave out the purple prose and the grandiose modifiers. If you say "market," be sure that everyone is talking about the same set of customers. If you say "profit," be sure to specify in what terms and where and when it will be measured. If you talk about "sales volume," be sure there is no misunderstanding about the point at which it is to be counted. If there is more than one way in which to interpret an objective, then there will be uncertainty in the means applied toward achieving the objective and, ultimately, an argument about whether or not the objective was actually attained.

The "Big Three"

Almost any business can define its criteria for success in a half dozen or fewer statements. There are three pretty standard "operating characteristic" criteria that almost all managements set: sales, earnings, and profitability. Beyond that they will set objectives dealing with the long-term structure and development of the company.

Sales

Almost every management looks for growth in volume. In most cases that means growth in dollar sales. There are kinds of enterprises where the sales-dollar figure is meaningless because of wide variations in prices or in amount of value added in manufacture, or because of other special characteristics. In this event a physical-volume criterion or some other point of measurement such as operating income will be much more significant.

If you choose a dollar sales-volume objective, set it in current dollars—which are what appear on your periodic operating statements—so that you can compare your performance directly against your objective from period to period without getting involved with the complication of price deflaters. However, this means that you have a built-in artificial growth due to price inflation. You have to decide at the time of setting the objective what amount of price inflation you are assuming. A lot of companies are now using 6 percent per year, and we will use that for our discussion purposes. If you have a good historical trend for your industry or for your company, one that gives you a different number, by all means use that.

In many markets you will also have to factor in a contrary trend of decreasing real prices as production costs follow a declining "learning curve" and the market becomes increasingly competitive. There are some theoretical equations for calculating such learning curves, but you may find that your past experience and feel for the market are more reliable in any specific instance. In every case that you set sales-volume objectives in current dollars, you are implying a price forecast. Write it down, either in actual prices or as an index. Then in future time periods, if prices deviate from your forecast, it will be very easy to adjust actual sales figures to see whether you are really staying on your objective line.

Most companies feel that they want to grow at least as fast as the national economy—that is, they don't want to become smaller relative to the entire industrial/commercial institution. The gross national product (GNP) is the most commonly used index of industrial activity; and if we take a growth rate of 4 percent per year in real GNP (that may be a little optimistic, but it makes the numbers come out even), we get a 10 percent per year annual growth rate in dollar sales just to stay even.

At this point you need your market analysis. If the market has been growing at 12 percent per year in current dollars, and you have no reason to believe that that trend will change, your sales will have to grow at 12 percent per year merely to maintain your share of the market. Remember that this means 6 percent per year in physical volume, since 6 percent represents price inflation. If you think that you can do better than your competition and increase your share of market, then the question is: Just how good do you think you are? Are there one or two "weak sister" competitors from whom you think you can steal present customers? How much of their business can you take over and how fast? Remember, you can only take those accounts over once, and therefore this tactic is not a source of continuous growth except to the extent that the newly won accounts continue to increase their demand.

In the likely event that any business you take away from your competitors will be more or less balanced by customers they win away from you, you will have to gain an increasing share of the market by preempting more than your share of its growth. Therefore, it is a useful trick to look at your planned increases in sales volume as percentages of growth in the market.

We have assumed that your market is growing at 12 percent per year. Let's say that you want to grow at 15 percent to double your volume in five years. The reasonableness of this objective depends in part on how much of the market you start with. If you have a modest 10 percent of the market, you could achieve the 15 percent growth rate by merely capturing about 13 percent of the new business and you would gain a modest one and one-half share points over the five-year period. On the other hand, if you start with 50 percent of the market, you would have to capture two-thirds of the new business and increase your market penetration to 57 percent by the end of a five-year period.

If you should presume to set as your objective a 20 percent annual growth in sales volume, it would mean that, if you started with 10 percent of the market, you would have to preempt 20 percent of the growth in a market growing at 12 percent per year. That may be feasible. But if you already have 50 percent of the market, you would have to capture virtually all the new business and would end up with over a 70 percent share. This sounds a little unrealistic, particularly since half of that market growth is simply price inflation (see Figure 6).

Of course, if your market were growing faster, it would all be much easier, which is why the first thing you look for when choosing new ventures to pursue is a rapidly growing market. If you come into a market cold and can capture 20 percent of its annual growth, you can reach that magic 10 percent participation level in less than four years, if the market is growing at 20 percent a year. But if the market is growing at only 5 percent a year (see Figure 7), it would take you 14 years to get that share if you performed just as well.

You can use the same curves for markets in which you already compete by adding your present share of market (SOM) to the incremental amount of the growth that you have to capture. Thus, if you already have 20 percent of a market, you have to get 20 percent of the market growth just to stay even. But if you can get 40 percent (20 + 20) of the growth in a market growing at 20 percent a year, you can pick up three share points in the first year and increase your participation by ten points up to 30 percent in the fourth year.

Figure 6. Relationship between market growth and sales growth.

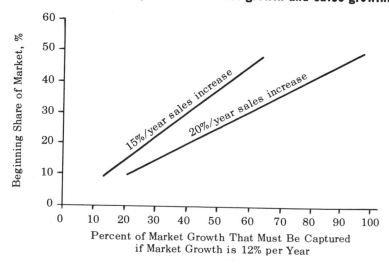

Figure 7. Effect of total market growth on market penetration.

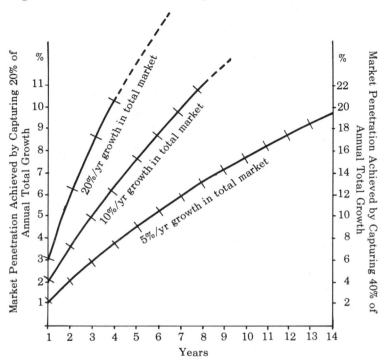

This is very important, since profitability is closely related to market share, as we will see later in this chapter.

These kinds of considerations will determine a reasonable sales-volume growth objective. The point is that you do not just pick a number because it sounds good to you or to the security analysts. You choose an objective relative to the magnitude of the opportunity that exists in the external environment. That objective will be influenced in great measure by what the total market is doing. To achieve a 15 percent annual growth in volume in a market that is growing at only 6 percent a year may be impossible if that 6 percent is all price inflation. Then there is really no new business out there for you to capture, so that any real growth you achieve will have to be gained at the expense of competitors who are already up against the wall. If you find yourself in this kind of bind, you had better go back and redefine your market.

What if you find that your market is declining? Often, one of the easiest situations in the world in which to show nice sales-volume growth is in a declining market because other people are getting out and you keep picking up their business. The trouble is that your sales growth will eventually come to a screeching halt and fall off precipitately when all the marginal suppliers are weeded out.

The people who are getting out of the market are getting out for a reason. There are lots of stupid people in this world, but you are only asking for trouble if you assume your competitors are among them. In a declining market the important questions are: How much time do you have to reorient yourself and reallocate your resources to get into something else? Who are the present suppliers to the market who are likely to drop out and give you a breathing spell? What are your volume/margin relationships? In other words, how long can you afford to go on before you stop making money in the market?

You can count on one thing: There probably will not be any new competitors in the market. It is also highly likely that no one is going to fight too hard to maintain a share of a declining market, which means that you may be able to improve your margins by cutting back on marketing expense, product development effort, and other promotional costs. The most important thing you want to do, though, is to start reallocating your corporate resources to activities with greater potential. There may be very little you can do with the fixed assets in plant and equipment, but one thing you can do is to start pulling your good people out of a wasting situation and try to get them into positions where they can exert some positive leverage on the future development of the enterprise. What you can do even before that is to call another mission session and reposition your business so that you stop trying to push water uphill.

The one thing you do not do is to set your objective on the basis of a sales forecast made by your existing sales force. This kind of forecast merely tells you what you can do if you keep doing the things you have been doing in the past, but a little more skillfully and a little more intensively. The sales forecast serves a different purpose. If you plot both the sales forecast and the objective line on the same graph, you can learn a great deal. If the sales forecast should be above the objective line and the objective has been intelligently set, then the only conclusion is that the sales people are living in a dream world and everyone is in for substantial disappointment. Usually, the forecast will fall below the objective line; the area between the two is called a "planning gap."

This planning gap will have to be filled with new tactics—things that you have not been doing in the past. Do not delude yourself into thinking that it can be filled by having people work harder, or avoiding the mistakes they've made in the past, or becoming cleverer. It very seldom works out that way. Your people are probably working about as hard as they can, and you are unlikely to find a reliable supplier of smart-pills. You will need new products, new marketing approaches, penetration into new market segments, improved product performance, or some other form of innovation to fill that gap. If you do not have specific innovative ideas in hand, you had better reduce that gap by scaling down the objective. Otherwise, you are likely to be in for some disappointment.

We have been assuming thus far that your business is such that you can view your market as a single entity even though you may segment it for more detailed planning. This is not always realistic. If you serve several discrete markets, you have two choices. You can have each of your product-group managers set his or her own objective and simply add them up, and *voilà*—a corporate sales objective! Or you can decide to *manage* the company.

In the latter case you might again start with the assumptions of a 6 percent annual inflation rate and a 4 percent annual GNP growth rate to give you a 10 percent, stay-even base line. But, you say, "We're better than the average company." Okay, but you have barely managed 5 percent per year *in constant dollars* over the past five years. Want to shoot for 6 percent real growth per year over the next five years? That would be 12 percent overall, including 6 percent price inflation, if there is no decline in *real* prices. "But we have been showing more than a 12 percent sales growth in *current* dollars. We can't afford to slack off. Furthermore, the leading company with which we compare ourselves has been chalking up 18 percent annual sales gains. We have to go for at least 15 percent."

All right, but remember: That is 9 percent real growth after the effects of price inflation, which is 50 percent better than the 5 to 6 percent you have been able to achieve in recent years. You are going to have to do a lot of things differently, not just better, than you have in the past. Remember, too, this objective is not just something to shoot at. If you set it, you are committed to achieving it, and you can count yourselves failures if you do not. Bye-bye bonus.

The point is that you set your growth objective in terms of just how good you think you are. Then you figure out how to prove it. If you expect to improve your real growth rate by 50 percent, it is unlikely you can do it with your present products in their present markets. If your product-group managers are both competent and honest, the sum of their sales objectives will probably fall short of that 15 percent line. That leaves you with a corporate planning gap.

You will have to fill the gap by corporate level initiative outside of the existing product divisions. You can do it overseas; you can do it by hyping up your new product development effort; you can set up a new division. But all these strategies will cost you money, which will give you trouble further along in the planning scheme. You can fill the gap by an acquisition, which in many respects is the easy way out, but that may be the toughest one to accommodate within your earnings and profitability objectives.

Earnings

If you could stop after merely setting a sales-volume objective, management would be a snap. Almost anyone can increase sales volume by going out and *buying* sales. You can do this with price concessions, but often you can accomplish it equally well by building "super" quality into the product, providing extraordinary customer services, using excessive advertising and promotion, or overpaying one or more segments of the distribution system.

Unfortunately, you also have to make a profit, at least in the long run and usually in the short run as well. You almost always have to buy growth, and you have to pay for it out of current earnings. The question is: How high a price are you willing to pay?

If you set your earnings-growth objective higher than your sales-growth objective—say 20 percent per year as related to the 15 percent annual growth in sales that we have been using as an example—it means that you are in a phase of "milking" the business. You are not growing as fast as you could by plowing earnings back into promotion and development, and you are opting to cash in, in the form of current earnings. You may find yourself in this position because you are consciously "disinvesting" in the business in order to redeploy assets elsewhere. You may be coming out of a promotional/developmental phase in which earnings were intentionally depressed by investment spending against potential future profits (not to be confused with capital investment in the accountant's sense).

You may believe that the sales-growth potential just is not there in the present circumstances and that additional sales increases could only be achieved at a prohibitive cost. You may be coming out of a period of depressed earnings brought about by excessive costs of production inputs, by destructive competition, or by mismanagement. You can find yourself in this situation in a very rapidly expanding market with very high sales-growth rates, where there is just no way to spend more money efficiently to stimulate greater growth. In any case you are not planning to plow back a constant proportion of your earnings into the business as your sales income increases.

If you are willing to accept a lower growth rate in earnings than in sales volume, you are declaring that you are still in a developmental phase. You are buying sales to increase your market, which will subsequently pay off in the long run. You are spending promotional money to establish brand franchises that will exist long into the future. You are investing in product development or organization development, in consumer education or some other form of investment spending over and above the level that would be justified by the existing sales income.

The one exception to this generality would be if your markets were growing very slowly—at or only slightly in excess of price inflation—and your earnings were virtually flat or declining because of the squeeze on your margins. If you "plan" that kind of situation very far into the future, you are not managing the company at all; you are letting it happen to you. You had better plan your way into a different situation because, otherwise, either you or your company (or conceivably both) are going to disappear from the industrial scene in due course.

At the corporate level you should set your objective in total dollar earnings after tax, less the effect of extraordinary items but including nonoperating income. This reflects the effectiveness of the total management, including the handling of tax matters, idle financial resources, and other items in addition to the management of operations. Division and other suborganizational earnings objectives should be set before taxes and before any other entries that are controlled at the corporate level and are thus beyond the influence of the divisional management.

A few companies like to look at total positive cash flow or even net cash flow, and these may be more significant numbers. In some businesses with weird depreciation situations, like some land developments, they are the only numbers that do have any significance. However, so few managers feel comfortable managing against cash flow criteria that the point is somewhat academic.

You do hear a lot about growth in earnings-per-share objectives. Of course if the number of shares outstanding stays the same, then the growth rate in earnings per share will be the same as the growth in dollar earnings, so the issue arises only when there is the prospect of a change in the equity structure. In fact, attention was only drawn to earnings per share criteria after some of the more rampant conglomerateurs in the 1950s and 1960s discovered that they could buy total earnings with stock certificates—"Chinese paper," as it came to be called. They would show impressive 40 and 50 percent growth in earnings, but would neglect to mention that the number of shares outstanding had doubled.

If you do plan to make a lot of acquisitions for stock, you might consider setting your earnings objective on a per-share basis, to keep yourself honest. However, that introduces problems too. If you float a new stock issue, the earnings per share will almost certainly drop, at least temporarily, and yet floating the issue may still be a very sound financing tactic.

Earnings per share really have more impact on stock price than anything else. If you get your executives running the company in the interest of maximizing the value of their stock options rather than enhancing the business, you have real troubles. There are legitimate situations in which you may want to buy earnings, and you may pay a premium price for them, but it will depress your per-share return.

If you are not going to do it too often, there are lots of ways to adjust an earnings objective for acquisitions. The simplest is to set the earnings objective for "present businesses" and to treat the earnings from acquisitions separately. Most important, if you hold hard on a return-on-assets objective, your dollar earnings figure can't lead you too far astray.

Keep it simple and watch total dollar earnings.

Profitability

A sales objective and an earnings objective still do not define the success of the business. If you throw enough assets indiscriminately into the enterprise, you can pump up both the earnings and the sales, but at an unacceptable resource cost. To say that a company is really well managed, we have to know whether its resources are being used effectively—how much net income is being produced by each dollar of resource at the management's disposal.

The simplest number to use is the return on total assets. There are some valid theoretical objections to this indicator, but they seem to be more acceptable than the biases of other available measures of profitability.

Some companies deduct the value of "intangible assets" (that is, goodwill) from the asset figure. Others add the imputed capital value of rented assets to the asset number. Both refinements have considerable justification.

A more controversial question is whether you should use gross assets—that is, before accumulated depreciation—or net assets—that is, the book value of depreciable assets. Both sides have credible arguments, but in comparing the company with itself from year to year, it makes very little difference which convention is used.

Similarly, there are various preferences as to just what to use as the numerator of the equation. Usually, interest is added to profits to make up the total return on assets. This is certainly theoretically sound, but if interest cost remains at approximately the same percentage of sales volume over the years, it behaves like any other variable cost and can be ignored in profitability calculations. Rents are also added into the numerator when leases are capitalized.

There are strong arguments for looking at profitability in terms of net return on equity, on the supposedly practical basis that this is what the business is all about—profitability to the owners. This argument is a little phony because the owners very seldom get their hands on all earnings and, except in a very young company, the equity figure on the balance sheet bears no relationship to what the stockholders actually invested in their ownership shares. Furthermore, this figure can bounce around if the pattern of financing is changed, without any real change in the quality of earnings.

Return on assets has the virtue of being the ultimate measure of the quality of earnings and therefore of the quality of management. It can be used at any level in the organization and related directly to the performance of most managers. Furthermore, it is simple. Therefore, we will set our objective in terms of

$$(\text{Net income after taxes})/(\text{book value of total assets})$$

It's not perfect, but it can't mislead us too much if we are honest about it, and it can be taken directly off the books. If you want to have a more sophisticated formula, by all means do.

You may not have so much freedom in setting your return-on-assets objective as you might think at first glance. You know intuitively that you must realize more than bank interest rates or the return on reasonably good-grade bonds. These are running at least 8 or 9 percent before taxes these days. However, closer to home, when you were setting policy in January, you may very well have made a statement about what you consider to be a prudent debt/equity ratio. At the same session you may have decided that, for various reasons, you have an obligation to your stockholders to pay out approximately a certain percentage of your earnings as dividends.

If you have set these two policies, you may have effectively locked yourself in. The amount of assets necessary to support a given sales volume is pretty much a characteristic of the kind of business you are in. Working capital tends to be directly proportional to sales volume and, over the long run, fixed investments will also increase at least as fast as sales volume, although possibly stepwise.

Given these conditions, there is a specific return on assets (ROA) that is necessary to support any particular sales growth. In your case you want a 15 percent annual growth of sales volume. Let's say equity represents half of the value of your total assets, you have decided that you should pay out about 40 percent of your earnings as dividends, and your depreciation funds are used entirely for equipment replacement. You need a 12.5 percent after-tax return on assets. If you cannot make that return, you cannot support your sales objective for many years unless you change some other factors. The equation looks like this:

$$\% \text{ ROA} = \frac{(\% \text{ sales growth per year}) \times (\text{equity/total assets}) \times 100}{\% \text{ earnings retained}}$$

Now, obviously, you can invert that equation to read

$$\% \text{ sales growth per year} = \frac{(\% \text{ ROA}) \times (\% \text{ earnings retained})}{(\text{equity/total assets}) \times 100}$$

This says that at a given rate of return, holding debt/equity and dividend payout ratios constant, you can determine the sales growth you can sustain over a period of years. Of course, in individual years, depreciation, cash flows, and variations in new fixed investment will cause the relationships to oscillate around this mean. Remember, too, we are using a return net *after*-interest payments, so that interest cost is treated like any other variable cost. Change in any cost that cannot be reflected in selling prices will impact directly on the ROA.*

On the basis of the numbers we have been assuming, if your traditional profitability has varied around 10 percent of assets employed, your internal cash flow plus your traditional pattern of outside financing can support only a 12 percent annual sales growth. You may as well be realistic and go back and change that sales objective *unless* you are willing to change the nature of your balance sheet or *unless* you have some very specific ideas on how to improve profitability. But wishing won't make it so. You will have to make fundamental changes if you are going to break out of your traditional profitability trend. This is where planning comes in. If you can *plan* such changes to improve profitability—then let's get at it.

However, plans to improve profitability are hard to come by. Competitive pressures tend to make rate of return a characteristic of a specific business or industry. If your profitability is below the average for your industry, it is almost certainly a sign of poor management. Get with it! On the other hand, if

---

* A more complicated equation, used by the Boston Consulting Group, is

$$g = \frac{d}{e}\,(r - i)\,p + rp$$

where g = rate of growth
       d = debt
       e = equity
       r = (profit + interest)/total assets
       i = interest rate
       p = percentage of earnings retained

   This equation does take into account the *effect* of interest cost, but becomes distorted if accounts payable are a substantial balance-sheet item since these are effectively interest-free financing.

your results are at or above the industry average, you probably will have to move into new venture areas with higher return characteristics if you are to make significant improvements.

Of course, if you are willing to change your financial policies, you can sustain that 15 percent annual growth in sales even with only a 10 percent ROA. If your stockholders will let you retain 75 percent of your earnings instead of 60 percent, you can do it (Figure 8). If you leverage up your balance sheet with additional debt so that your equity amounts to less than 40 percent of your total assets, you can do it. On the other hand, if you were not so highly leveraged, you might not be able to sustain 15 percent annual sales growth at all.

The net margin or return on sales (ROS) that you will have to realize will depend on how many times a year you can turn over your assets. That equation looks like this:

$$\% \text{ net margin (ROS)} = \frac{(\% \text{ ROA}) \times (\text{total assets})}{\text{sales volume}}$$

You can set a return on sales objective if you want because it is a very easy one to monitor, but it won't really contribute anything additional to your definition of the business because it is already determined by the other objectives you have set. Furthermore, if you have a diversity of product lines, the overall corporate average ROS may be meaningless because the data for every product line will be different.

Development Objectives

Having set the "big three" primary objectives for sales, earnings, and profitability, you have pretty well characterized the business in terms of ongoing financial operating results. However, except in the very narrowest banker's sense, you have done very little about assuring the long-term vitality of the enterprise or about minimizing its vulnerability to unexpected, unsettling events over which you have no control.

If you concentrate on these three objectives and set up your control system to police them, you will end up with a very

Figure 8. Dependence of sales growth on ROA.

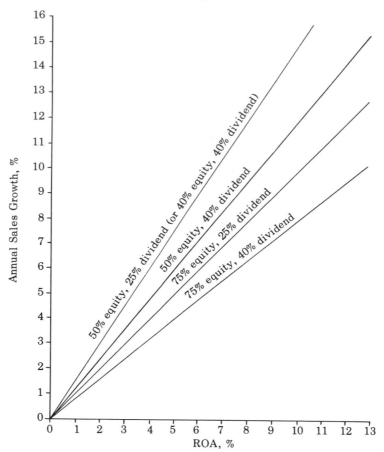

short-range management despite your fine sentiments about long-range strategies. These are dimensions that can be managed from day to day, so your managers will get the message that you are interested only in short-range operating figures. They will expect to be rewarded on the basis of their short-term operating performance, and that is where they will focus their time and attention.

Therefore, you must include in your plan some primary objectives aimed specifically at the future development of the enterprise. These objectives must have equal status with the "big three." You have to be sure to convince everyone that it is essential to fulfill *all* primary objectives if the management is to consider itself successful.

As in the instances we have discussed so far, attaining these additional development objectives is going to make it harder to reach the first three objectives. They will cost money that will have to be expensed. They will divert resources, particularly staff time and effort, from the direct sales effort. They may very well require capital investment that will not be immediately productive.

It is exactly this tension and balance among your primary objectives that set the strategy for your firm. How much growth and in what direction at what cost for what investment, and where do you hope to get to next? You have to do all these things equally well if you are to attain that strong strategic thrust. Five out of six is not pretty good. Five out of six is like coming in second in a boxing match.

Development objectives are very peculiar to any given business and cannot be broadly generalized. However, I can give you some suggestions.

One candidate that you certainly should consider is an objective to attain or hold a certain share of the market which is the backbone of your business. The chapter on mission said that if you do not have as much as 10 percent of the market, in most businesses you are going to be scrambling. But beyond that, there is an almost magic correlation between share of market (SOM) and profitability (ROA). There is an ongoing study at the Marketing Science Institute at Harvard Business School that has thus far analyzed 620 businesses with wide diversity of markets. On the average, a difference of ten percentage points in market share produces a 5 percent difference in pretax ROI.*

* In this project, ROI is defined as pretax operating profit plus interest divided by equity plus long-term debt. This formulation avoids the problems of dealing with current liabilities as part of the financial structure. The basic relationship between market share and profitability is not significantly different than it would be if return on assets (ROA) were used.

As you can see from Figure 9, at market shares below 10 percent, pretax return tends to drop below 10 percent whereas at 50 percent share of market (SOM), average return is about 30 percent. There are a lot of theories offered to explain why this relationship exists, not the least credible of which is that good management produces *both* high profitability and high market share. Whatever the reason, the phenomenon exists, and it is worth taking into account as you plan your corporate strategy.

You should also remember that "market" is a fairly flexible term, and therefore so is "share of market." You can define your market almost arbitrarily, and by limiting the service area in which you choose to compete, you can manipulate your SOM up to a level at which you can enjoy the benefits of a substantial market share. Of course you can cheat on this, too, and just juggle words, but if you do it honestly and consequently avoid scattering your shots, the payoff is there.

There may seem to be some overlap between your sales objective and an SOM objective, but the perspective is different. Here you are saying that although you want sales growth, you don't want just any old sales but that you want to concentrate your sales effort in your areas of maximum market strength.

Figure 9. Relationship between market share and pretax ROI.

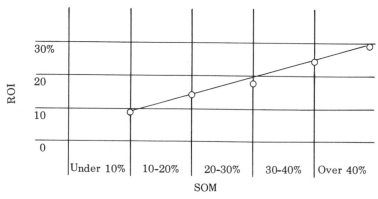

Reprinted with permission from *Harvard Business Review*.

If you are a high-technology industry or one in which there is a high rate of product obsolescence, you will undoubtedly want to set an objective for research and development performance. You may merely declare your intention to always have the highest performance unit in the field. That is not quantitative, but it is specific in that (if you are reasonably honest with yourself) there will be little question as to whether yours is the best or not. This kind of objective will make it tougher to achieve your earnings objective. You may set an objective in terms of the frequency of new product introductions. You may set as an objective the intention to be able to duplicate any technological innovation by a competitor within six months or a year, or within some specific time period after it hits the market.

Please do not set as an objective "to spend x percent of sales income on research/development programs." This only assures that you will spend a certain amount of money and says nothing about results. It describes an action, not an objective.

You may wish to set an objective to consciously expand your market. A retailer might set an objective in terms of store openings, or someone else might decide to expand into new geographical regions on a regular schedule or to achieve national distribution by the end of the planning period. Another organization might set special objectives in growth of export sales or of international activity. A heavy equipment manufacturer might set a primary objective in terms of order backlog. A professional services organization might be specifically concerned with expanding into new fields of competence by recruiting additional talent.

Organizations are frequently concerned about overdependence on a single customer or a single market, and will set objectives to reduce their dependence on that market by concentrating their growth in other areas. Suppliers to the military are frequently in this position, but so are suppliers to the automotive industry and manufacturers for large retail chains. This kind of objective, though common, is very hard to manage because it is essentially negative. In some cases it may entail finding alternative uses for facilities currently occupied in a low-profit business. More frequently, though, it entails denying promotional expenses to one segment of the business and allocating those funds preferentially to another area. It could involve a period of forced growth in other areas of the business to bring the balance into more tolerable limits. Such forced growth is always costly and could require renegotiating the earnings objective.

There is another kind of negative objective you should definitely consider. An old business maxim is, "The best way to make money is to stop losing it." Should you set an objective to eliminate over a period of time all products that do not meet some business performance criterion? You can set your cutoff criterion in terms of gross margin, or ROA, or SOM, or whatever is most appropriate. The point is to shuck your losers. Every organization has got to have a bottom drain. If you don't draw off the gunk once in a while, the system will fill up with sludge and there just won't be enough reaction space left to sustain the process. It is amazing how few managements perform this function well. It takes tremendous discipline exercised down through layers of managers. Maybe you should make it a primary objective to see that it gets done.

When you get your set of primary objectives completed, they will tell you—and anyone else who has the occasion to read them—a great deal about how you intend to pursue the business of your company. They will reflect a distillation of your best strategic thinking about just what is the optimum balance between growth and profits, risk and security, expansion and concentration. This is not a job to be undertaken lightly. It is unlikely that you will ever be faced with more important management decisions during your stewardship of the company's affairs.

One of the most interested audiences for your primary objectives will be your board of directors. They should be much more concerned with these ultimate results than they will be with any of the subsequent details of the plan.

Get your finance department to prepare a simple exhibit showing the yearly consequences through the planning period of the objectives you have set for yourself. This should not be a complete balance sheet and cash flow forecast. Concentrate on the critical values that the board members will be most interested in, such as earnings per share, probable financing schedules, and dividend payout.

Present the exhibit to the board of directors and explain that although its contents are *pro forma* at this point, unless subsequent investigation proves these objectives to be unrealistic, you fully intend to achieve this pattern of accomplishment. Point out that this is not yet a plan but rather is an explicit way of outlining the basic strategy you intend to pursue. The nature of your development objectives should tell them more clearly than any amount of narrative language just where you are heading the company.

If they feel that you are planning to move too fast or too slowly, that you are sacrificing current earnings too drastically or are being insufficiently imaginative in seeking reinvestment opportunities, now is the time to speak up. You may as well find where you stand before you put a lot of work into detailed planning.

Because the set of primary objectives is so fundamental to the way in which the business is going to be run, it is important that any manager with anything like policy responsibility should know what they are and be regularly reminded that this is where the company is going. Of course it can be embarrassing to the top management if the objectives are consistently missed, but maybe even that is good. Put the primary objectives in everybody's planning book right after the mission and strategic policies.

SUGGESTED READING

Anonymous, *Return on Capital as a Guide to Managerial Decisions.* New York: National Association of Accountants, 1959.

An excellent discussion of the variations of ROI calculations and how to use them.

Buzzell, R. D., Gale, B. T., and Sultan, R. G. M., "Market Share —A Key to Profitability," *Harvard Business Review*, Vol. 53, No. 1 (January–February 1975).

Current findings from the Marketing Science Institute ongoing study.

Davis, James V., "The Strategic Divestment Decision," *Long Range Planning*, Vol. 7, No. 1 (February 1974).

On when and how to get out of a business.

Granger, C. H., "How to Set Company Objectives," *Management Review*, Vol. 59 (July 1970).

Good basics.

Hayes, Robert H., "New Emphasis on Divestment Opportunities," *Harvard Business Review*, Vol. 50, No. 4 (July–August 1972).

How to win with losers.

Jain, S., "Translating Experience into Growth," *Managerial Planning*, Vol. 23, No. 5 (March–April 1975), pp. 1–5.

Some comments on experience curves and a case study of a rather spectacular application of the theory to a product/marketing plan.

Ketrick, J. C., "A Formal Model for Long-Range Planning, Part 1," *Long Range Planning*, Vol. 1, No. 3 (March 1969).

Another approach to calculating the interaction between rate of earnings and potential for growth.

Schoeffler, S., Buzzell, R. D., and Heany, D. F., "Impact of Strategic Planning on Profit Performance," *Harvard Business Review*, Vol. 52, No. 2 (March–April 1974).

Additional findings from the Marketing Science Institute study show that the profit impact of marketing expenditures, research ex-

penditures, product quality, investment intensity, and company size all vary relative to market share.

Searby, F. W., "Return to Return on Investment," *Harvard Business Review*, Vol. 53, No. 2 (March–April 1975).

Some ideas on improving profitability.

Steiner, G. A., *Top Management Planning.* New York: The Macmillan Company, 1969, chap. 13.

Discussion of various forms of ROI calculation.

7

The Difficult
You Do Immediately

Do what you can, with what you have, where you are.
T. ROOSEVELT

YOUR primary objectives define the balance and direction that
you propose for the development of the enterprise during the
planning period. The next task is to begin to fill in the details.
You will want to get your marketing plan in the works immediately, as discussed in Chapter 8, but you already have some
component parts in the works that you can begin to deal with
while the marketing plan is in preparation.

Threats and Opportunities

When you did your environmental analysis, you requested
action-plan proposals to respond to critical threats and opportunities that you identified in the general environment. Some
of these assignments were subsequently absorbed into projects

relating to strengths and weaknesses, but the remainder should be coming in about now.

In the cases involving environmental threats that could have a possible serious negative impact on your business you will have to make a judgment. Is the threat as real and as imminent as you thought? Can you afford the cost required to protect yourself against it? How much exposure are you willing to risk? Then you decide: Will you or must you accept the risk? If you decide that you will or must accept the risk, you put the proposal aside as a contingency plan or discard it entirely as impracticable. If you are unwilling to hazard the chance, you must approve the plan for implementation. Your decision will inevitably be subjective and will reflect your attitude toward risk. Are you willing to "bet the company," or do you want your flanks covered? If you commit resources—particularly people—to these protective programs, you won't have them for more aggressive activities.

If you decide that you must protect yourself, initiate the programs right away. If you are going to do it, you may as well get started. No need to wait until the "plan" is finished.

The programs proposed to exploit opportunities do not require immediate decision. You need to give them careful consideration. Be sure you understand the magnitude and probabilities of the opportunities, and agree with the approach proposed and with the magnitude of the effort outlined. You don't know yet what resources you will have available for such offensive excursions or how they would fit in with your overall plans. So these proposals are tabled to provide a kind of idea inventory for the subsequent planning steps.

Some of the proposals may be picked up in the marketing plan or even the facilities plan. Most likely some will be subsumed under one of the development objectives. If there are any left "unclaimed" by the end of the planning process, they might be adopted by a corporate development function to fill any remaining planning gap or as low-priority, backup development plans.

Unfortunately, however, in the real world, you are most likely to run out of resources before you can arrange to take advantage of all your opportunities. That is, if your people have any imagination and insight, you will. Then you have to start looking for resources you can reallocate from less productive uses in order to take advantage of the opportunity. Since you know what you are looking for, the planning process should give you a good chance of finding them. If you do find them, don't lose your nerve. Pull them out no matter how venerable their niche and put them where the action is.

Strengths and Weaknesses

Proposed programs to eliminate weaknesses should also be coming in because you asked that these be tackled on a crash basis. Take whatever time it takes to agree that you have the optimal program to eliminate the weakness in the shortest possible time, and get the thing moving. In some cases you may even get the situation cleaned up before your next planning period starts. Probably it won't be that easy, but get it done as soon as possible—if you don't, all the planning you are going to do in the rest of the year may be a waste of time.

Your proposals to exploit strengths will be a little slower in coming in, both because they do not have the urgency and because the target is not so clearly defined. If you had some good sharp minds on these jobs, some of the proposals may be so obviously advantageous that you might as well implement them right away. You know that programs based on already existing capabilities are going to get a high priority because they have the greatest probability of success. So as fast as you can get the resources together, you might as well get started on the really promising ones. If some of the proposed projects are more problematical, you can add them to the "opportunities" programs in the stockpile of ideas for possible inclusion in the developing plan. They really will have to compete with those proposals for resources still available at the end of the planning cycle.

SUGGESTED READING

Gameroni, D., "Resource Appraisal: An Early Warning System for the Board," *Director* (March 1969), pp. 377–380.

Description of a technique for detecting operational weaknesses and incorporating them into long-range plans.

Hussey, D. E., "The Corporate Appraisal: Assessing the Company Strengths and Weaknesses, *Long Range Planning*, Vol. 1, No. 2 (April 1968), pp. 19–25.

Treatment in depth of this phase of the long-range planning process.

8
How Are You Going to Get There?

It is not enough to be busy . . . the question is: What are we busy about?
THOREAU

THE primary objectives are the backbone of your plan. Everything that you do from now on should contribute to one or more of these objectives, or you should just not do it. However, the primary objectives are so fundamental that are very hard to get a grip on. How do you go about increasing earnings by 15 percent a year or assuring a 12.5 percent return on assets? You have to break them down into more manageable units.

A chief executive officer is personally and directly responsible for the accomplishment of the primary corporate objectives. Any other responsible executive has a comparable set of objectives for which he or she is primarily responsible. From here on out you will want to parcel out the responsibility for subcomponents to other members of your organization. Before taking the next step, you will have to work on each one of the primary objectives separately and then bring them back together to see whether they are mutually compatible.

Depending on how you are organized, you may be able to work on each of the "Big Three" operating objectives with a separate team: sales and marketing on the sales objective, production on the earnings objective, the financial people on the return-on-assets objective. However, there are considerable advantages in having your whole team participate across the board. It is likely to save time in the long run. It certainly will improve communications, and by assuring a broader perspective on individual aspects as they come up, you usually eliminate some false starts and blind alleys. As a compromise in this discussion, we will have the total planning team act as a review body, and organizational units or task forces will do the preliminary details.

Assign one of your immediate subordinates responsibility for preparing a program proposal for each of the development objectives. The choice of the individual will usually be fairly automatic because of the nature of the objective. However, you may wish to make ad hoc appointments to the subordinate's task force from outside the normal organizational relationships. You will want to be an ex officio member of each of these task forces and take a more or less active role as your schedule and disposition suggest. You can lead one or more of the task forces if you choose. At this point, these task forces may absorb one or more of the teams set up to exploit a particular strength, if you have decided to make the exploitation of that strength an indepdendent primary objective.

What you want from each task force is an analysis of the problem of achieving the objective and a broad-brush proposal on the way it should be attacked. This must include breaking the problem down into a hierarchy of objectives in the manner discussed in Chapter 9. You need a timetable and a rough budget covering expenses, investments, and personnel requirements. You also want to know whether to expect any sales and/or earnings benefits from the programs during the planning period. This job will require considerable thought but not much paper to get it written down. Put some good people on the job. These development objectives have the greatest leverage in determining the long-term strategic posture of the enterprise.

The Marketing Plan

When you get your development task forces set up, the next thing you need to do is get the sales and marketing people to give you a marketing plan. This is not a sales forecast but an expression of their best judgment as to where they would expect to generate the sales volume to achieve the target growth rate over the coming years. This can be done by geographical regions, or by products, or by market segments, or in any matrix that makes most sense to them. If they are going to need new products or new product performance, they should say so.

They should give both dollar figures and physical volume figures, which means that they will have to make a price forecast in current dollars. This implies a pricing strategy. Be sure they write it down and put it in the plan so that everybody knows what assumptions they are using. They should have a general idea of the marketing budgets that are going to be required and of the personnel they will need. They may also incorporate input from work already done by a "strength" or "opportunity" team.

You do not want a highly detailed document with lots and lots of spread sheets. Relatively few pages should be sufficient. What you are after is a plus-or-minus 10 percent type of figure that will illuminate their marketing strategy. You want to know where they think the big opportunities are, where they intend to concentrate their resources, what markets they are going to fight for, and which ones they feel have little or no potential. In other words, you want the subobjectives that must be attained in order to add up to the sales growth you have agreed you will achieve, supported by the reasons for segmenting the objective in this particular way.

The marketing plan should reflect the observations and assumptions they have made about what is going to happen in the total markets in which you compete. It had better also reflect a realistic appreciation of the analysis of your competitors, which you did previously.

When the marketing plan has been completed—and it should not take more than two months—have it distributed to the planning group. People should have some time to chew on it and, if possible, digest it before a presentation is made. If your marketing and sales people are any good, they're going to be pretty glib. It will be only too easy for them to get away with a snow job if everyone has to field his or her ideas cold. Set a meeting date between one and two weeks after the distribution. At that meeting have the marketing people present, and have them explain and defend their proposed plan. Take a whole day for this because if this is done superficially and received with a nod of acquiescence, nothing else will hang together tightly. See that the marketing people get a good grilling.

If your production people and financial people and other functional executives are relatively naive about what is going on in the market, they had better start learning now. As senior executives, they must appreciate that what happens on the selling line will ultimately determine the success of the business. The customer's needs and how he or she perceives your company's product relative to those needs are ultimately the sovereign determinant of corporate success.

If the marketing plan is not convincing, if the marketing people cannot project their rationale, if there are missing links in their logic, or if they are depending on miracles from production or product development, which their colleagues are just not willing to guarantee, then the plan has to go back to the drawing board. It is better to delay your planning cycle than to continue to go through the motions when there is no confidence in the underlying premises.

You want to avoid both "We sold it, now you make it!" and "We made it, now you sell it!" Both attitudes are self-defeating. What you want is a single system that starts with the function you provide to your customer and leads to the optimal disposition of the resources at your disposal to do the best possible job of providing that function economically. The marketing and sales people cannot attain a sales objective by themselves. They need product performance, quality assurance, production capability, financial support—in fact, they need the help of every part of the organization. They are the best ones to tell you how the market will react, but the commitment to sales performance has to come from the entire group.

You may, however, run into a direct difference of opinion—even a personality opposition—of the "Yes, I can." No, you can't" type. Production men, for instance, sometimes fancy themselves quite expert on marketing. In that case it must be made crystal clear to *all* parties that the marketing/sales people are, after all, the specialists in that area. They are staking their professional reputations as well as their hope of future bonuses on their ability to perform according to plan. This is their contract, and if they fail to perform to the specifications, they are in default. If no one can find a fault in their logic, if there is no specific substantive reason why their plan can be proved faulty, then it must be accepted.

Once the marketing plan is accepted, everyone else must then proceed to lay the plans for his or her respective area of responsibility on the assumption that the sales objective will be achieved. This means that R&D is committed to develop the products required by the plan. Production is committed to have manufacturing capacity. Quality will be acceptable. Deliveries will be made as scheduled. Customer credit must be available. If there is any equivocation at this point, if other functional areas independently discount the sales plan, you will have chaos and a long history of reciprocal recriminations.

The marketing plan must include a price projection. The marketing people will propose one, but the rest of you old-timers should have some pretty solid opinions about its reasonableness. If marketing predicts a steady price in constant dollars—that is, without inflationary effect—look out. Real prices tend to decline, except in a business in which nobody is making any money—and you should not be in that kind of business anyway. There is a lot of theory to support this contention (learning curves and such), but if you have been around very long, you know in your gut this is so. Don't kid yourself. The only question is, "How fast, how far?" You have to guess, but factor it into your plans anyhow.

After you forecast an industry price trend, you still have to decide what your *pricing strategy* is going to be. Are you going to meet prevailing prices? Be price-aggressive competitors? Hold a premium price? Your pricing strategy affects your projected operating statement, but it must be compatible with your share-of-the-market (SOM) expectations, your marketing expense allocation, your product development program, and probably manufacuring as well.

The Production/Facilities Plan

Once the marketing plan is accepted, it is the turn of your production, facilities, and engineering people to tell you what it is going to cost to produce this material. If you are a service rather than a manufacturing concern, you will have to go through the same steps, although the terms will be slightly different.

Production people will have to forecast raw material prices, unless you are in a position where changes in raw material costs can always be passed directly through to the customer in the selling price. They will have to make some assumptions about labor costs and the costs of other factors of production. They will have to think about productivity and the seasonal cycles of production. And, of course, they will have to predict the need for new fixed investment in manufacturing and/or distribution facilities.

When they are ready—and presumably they will get started while the marketing plan is still being put together—it is their turn to be put on the spot for a presentation and defense of their plan. The amount of time you allow for this will depend to some extent on the complexity and centrality of your manufacturing operation. However, don't try to get by with an hour or slip it in at the end of your regular management committee meeting. Set up a special occasion, and take at least half a day.

At this point you don't want plant designs or detailed production schedules or a lot of production cost data, although somebody undoubtedly will have to do a lot of calculator work before the plan is put together. What you want to know is the overall approach that will be taken to assure there will be adequate product in quantity, quality, and kind to meet the sales pattern that the sales department says it can move. You also want to know what this will cost.

Now is the time for sales to scream for adequate inventories to prevent back orders and for the treasurer to scream right back at them that it costs too much. This is where the tradeoff should be hammered out between the high productivity of long production runs and the necessity to have a broad product line and to provide prompt delivery. If new capacity is to be installed, what kind and how much and where? This is not a decision that production and engineering can make alone.

The first time you do this analysis you may have to recycle the production/facilities plan. Hopefully, with a little experience, the people responsible for these functional plans will learn to consult with people in other areas of the organization before they get too far along so that when they finally get it all put together they will not have big surprises.

The first time and the second time and probably every other time you review the facilities plan, you will have to be alert for overbuilt facilities. "Goldplating" with excessive instrumentation, deluxe exteriors, and unwarranted redundancy in equipment is sometimes hard to spot, particularly if only the production management is technically trained. If you cannot get comparative figures from similar installations to use as guidelines, maybe you should have an independent technical adviser go over the facilities figures with you.

However, these technicalities are not likely to be the major problem. Engineers are primarily trained to think in terms of production efficiency: labor productivity, raw material conversion, and—now more frequently—energy efficiency. They seldom consider capital productivity. An old plant is usually less "efficient," and anyhow it is not so much fun to run as a new plant with all the latest whistles and bells. A second or third shift is not going to be so "productive" as the first shift, and it is more trouble to supervise. Pushing a unit hard against or beyond its rated capacity will usually cut down the material-conversion rate.

All these tactics will increase unit costs and cut operating margins. Furthermore, they are not neat. But you can stand a little higher unit cost—maybe quite a bit higher—if you can avoid or even defer a lot of new fixed investment for which you are going to have to generate a financial return. Be sure that you are getting as much production volume as possible—not just comfortable—out of your existing plant before you plan any new capacity.

Figure 10 represents the kind of analysis that too frequently is *not* done. Too often production people shoot for maximum output at minimum variable cost per unit, which in this example occurs at one shift per day for a five-day week. But even if we assume that variable unit cost goes up very sharply after that point because of loss of efficiency, high rejects, night shift or overtime premiums, and so forth, the minimum total cost per unit is not exceeded until we get over 12 shifts per week (two six-day shifts).

But not even this is the optimum economic point at which to run the plant. It will still make some incremental cash contribution until you get beyond 18 shifts per week (three six-day shifts) even though by that time your variable unit costs are over twice the minimum. And you still have more than a 10 percent capacity cushion that you can use, for limited periods at least, to hold your market if you underestimate your requirements. Of course you may have to block out some time for clean-out and turnaround or to plan against peak seasonal demand rather than year-round average, but the principle is the same.

Before you plan on new capacity, see that this kind of analysis is made so that you don't build anything before you

Figure 10. Model production-unit capacity analysis.

Critical Points	Units	Manufacturing Costs — Fixed	Variable Unit	Total	Average per Unit — Cost	Contribution	Marginal Unit — Cost	Contribution	Total Contribution	Fixed Assets	Contribution Fixed Assets
	10	100	1.0	110	11.0	−7.0		3.0	−70	100	−0.70
	20	100	1.0	120	6.0	−2.0	1.0	3.0	−40	100	−0.40
Plant break-even ↑	30	100	1.0	130	4.3	−0.3	1.0	3.0	−10	100	−0.10
	40	100	1.0	140	3.5	0.5	1.0	3.0	20	100	0.20
	50	100	1.0	150	3.0	1.0	1.0	3.0	50	100	0.50
	60	100	1.1	166	2.8	1.2	1.6	2.4	74	100	0.74
Minimum variable	70	100	1.2	184	2.6	1.4	1.8	2.2	96	100	0.96
cost/unit (five shifts/ ↑	80	100	1.3	204	2.55	1.45	2.0	2.0	116	100	1.16
week)	90	100	1.4	226	2.5	1.5	2.2	1.8	134	100	1.34
	100	100	1.5	250	2.5	1.5	2.4	1.6	150	100	1.50
	110	100	1.6	276	2.5	1.5	2.6	1.4	164	100	1.64
Minimum total cost/	120	100	1.7	304	2.5	1.5	2.8	1.2	176	100	1.76
unit (12½ shifts/week) ↑	130	100	1.8	334	2.6	1.4	3.0	1.0	186	100	1.86
	140	100	1.9	366	2.6	1.4	3.2	0.8	194	100	1.94
	150	100	2.0	400	2.7	1.3	3.4	0.6	200	100	2.00
	160	100	2.1	436	2.7	1.3	3.6	0.4	204	100	2.04
Maximum contribution ↑	170	100	2.2	474	2.8	1.2	3.8	0.2	206	100	2.06
	180	100	2.3	514	2.9	1.1	4.0	0.0	206	100	2.06
	190	100	2.4	556	2.9	1.1	4.2	−0.2	204	100	2.04
	200	100	2.5	600	3.0	1.0	4.4	−0.4	200	100	2.00
Absolute capacity (21 shifts/week) ↑	210	100	2.6	646	3.1	0.9	4.6	−0.6	194	100	1.94

Pro Forma Standard Costs per Unit.

Manufacturing cost 2.5
Marketing and distribution 1.0

Contribution
Allocated costs   0.5
Profit B/T   1.0
Total sales price   5.0

really need to. It is not that the engineers are trying to con you. It's just that they don't instinctively *think* profitability.

Don't let the accountants run the production department, but do insist that your production management keep its eye on that ROA and not just on the monthly operating statement.

After you have educated them a little bit, they may get cagey and start to argue that construction costs are going up faster than the interest cost of money; therefore, even if you build the new plant too soon, you still save money. This argument is a little harder to handle, partly because they might be right. The problem is essentially one of risk. Are you willing to tie up your capital unnecessarily in process equipment that inevitably will someday be obsolescent to produce a product that someday will lose favor in the market? It depends on how far out you think those "somedays" are.

Do take your production people's word for what to do about plant safety and environmental controls. If they need legal advice, get it for them. They should be clearly responsible in these areas for keeping you out of court. But if you are going to hold them responsible, you have to do what they say. Don't get into the spot where they get on a witness stand and have to say, no matter how reluctantly, "Well, I told them to do it, but they didn't want to spend the money."

If you have a separate design engineering department, you are going to have another problem with your facilities plan. Better have it at the planning table, though, than have a lot of bickering and buck passing after the plant is built. "Sure the process worked when it was run by a bunch of engineers, but I have to work with green operators." "If they would only read the meters and follow the operating manual, they wouldn't have down time." And on and on.

Actually, you won't get into design details in strategy sessions—or you shouldn't anyhow—but the principle should be established right at the beginning and right at the top. Production has got to make the plant work. No question! But since it is production's figurative neck that will ultimately be stretched, the production people have to insist that the planned design is operable in the real world. This means that they have to intrude upon the design process, whether they are invited or not. It does nobody any good for them to say when the illegitimate baby is left on their doorstep, "I didn't do it!" Be sure they understand from the earliest planning stages that they *must* make the plant work. They will not be allowed to pass the buck. And be sure the design department knows it, too. The same thing applies to distribution people and distribution facilities.

You may have still another problem in getting a good production/facilities plan. Your production people may be reluctant to predict production costs. Understandable. It's a tough game. But who is better qualified to do it if they don't? The cost accountants? Heaven help you!

Sure, production people will need some inputs from personnel. They will certainly need to work with purchasing, and here you may have to let them off the hook somewhat if you deal with a cost-volatile raw material. Let them forecast conversion costs. They had better look back at that competitive analysis, too, before they submit their final numbers.

Once there is general agreement on the production/facilities plan, you will have a first indication of how well you are accomplishing your earnings objective. You have your marketing budget from the marketing plan, your manufacturing costs from production. You should have a pretty good idea of what your overhead burden rates are. You have a price forecast. If the earnings projections are within sight of your objective line, you can tell people to start thinking of ways that earnings can be improved and go on to the next step.

If earnings are way out of line, you had better stop right here and begin to reconsider the marketing plan and the facilities plan to see where you can make some structural changes to get back in the ball park. This can be tough, but it's no use to continue to delude yourself that you have a viable strategy if you've landed in a blind alley.

You may have to forgo some new product introductions or some market extensions. You may have to work the plants harder by adding more shifts or increasing the length of the workweek in order to spread the fixed costs. You may have to forgo serving some peak seasonal demands in order to improve the load factor on your plant. No matter what you have to do to compensate, get yourself a basic structure that has some chance of achieving your objectives. We are still at the rough-cut stage here, but you should at least be on your earnings growth curve—certainly not more than 25 percent below it—because you will have to add some additional expenses to the plan before we get through.

Profitability Forecast I

If you do have a reasonable first cut at the earnings performance, ask your finance department to forecast a trial return on assets (ROA). They know from the facilities plan approximately what the fixed asset requirements will be, with possible additions for nonproductive facilities (such as office buildings and parking lots) that are under consideration in other parts of the organization. The finance people can derive from past experience approximately how much additional working capital will be required for expanded sales. They can divide the forecast of total assets into the 15 percent annual earnings growth line, year by year. If you cannot hold the required ROA level at the objective line, you are committing too much capital to develop the business. You will have to reduce the resource requirements or accept a lower ROA.

It is possible that you can make substantial reductions in asset requirements by a revised inventory policy, better cash management, or a revised credit policy. It is much more likely that the only place you can make important reductions is in fixed investment. Are you really working these plants as hard as they will go? How much profit are you likely to lose by deferring that plant expansion for a year? Do you really need that new office building or employee canteen?

If you can still see daylight after you have your preliminary marketing, production, and profitability plans in hand, it is worthwhile to proceed with more detailed planning. Schedule a series of presentations by the task forces assigned to your development objectives. Allow half a day for each presentation. You can call them consecutively if you want.

The first order of business is to critique the logic with which the task forces have approached the problem and the magnitude of their budget numbers. Is their analysis of the problem sound? Have they broken it down into subobjectives in the most productive pattern? Is the rate of progress they predict reasonably attainable? Are there sufficient resources available to do the job?

Continue the examination until your planning team agrees that the approach is optimal and that the cost and benefit figures are approximately correct. Then reaffirm your responsibility for the primary objective and confirm responsibility of other individuals for each of the subobjectives.

These development objectives are in addition to, or parallel to, the current operating statement objectives we have been dealing with. Their impact is additive and any sales and earnings they generate should be added to the marketing plan and the earnings projection. However, sales and earnings as such are not the reasons for these objectives. They may entail additional capitalized investment, which must be added to that in the profitability forecast. They certainly will involve expenses that will be charged currently and that will depress current earnings accordingly.

Profitability Forecast II

Ask your finance department to recast its financial projections to incorporate the programs for development objectives and to include any costs and benefits from any of the programs you have already initiated as the result of your environmental and operational analyses. This time you want your financial people to do a *pro forma* profit-and-loss statement to see what this is all adding up to.

At this point you are beginning to have the rough outlines of a plan. It is a sort of basted fit. If it really looks feasible, you are ready to start stitching the pieces together and work on the detailing.

If this second profitability forecast seems to be within gun range, you can now shoot for your profitability objective. You can't really do it before this—not because it is not important, but because you don't know what the problem is. If your forecast shows a completely unacceptable profitability (say, 5 or 6 percent ROA), you will have to recycle the plan completely. You will have to find a way to pull some expenses out, or to increase margins substantially, or to change somehow the financial characteristics of your business. There is no point in going ahead on *planning* yourself into an unacceptable position.

However, if your rough-cut analysis shows you a 9 or 10 percent ROA, you may have a manageable "planning gap." This is everybody's responsibility, and everybody can contribute to the solution. Get the gang together and see what it can come up with. Don't count too much on "saving paper clips." If you can pick up a couple of points of ROA by conventional cost-cutting programs, you have a pretty sloppy operation.

Remember, there are two ways to boost ROA. One is to increase income; the other is to reduce assets employed. One is just as good as the other. You should be able to make gains at both ends. If you can reduce your asset base, you usually win both ways because you save interest cost.

This has to be a real shirt-sleeve session. Good intentions won't do. You need specific programs to produce specific results. Start with the earnings-growth objective. How far are your projected earnings from that 15 percent growth objective line? If the projections and the objective line are practically identical, then you know where your problem is. You have too much investment. More likely the earnings projections fall short of the objective. You have a planning gap, and you know just how big it is and when.

What specific subobjectives can you realistically propose to close up that gap? Cut corporate overhead? How much? How soon? For how long? Raise prices? Which ones? How much will it cost in sales? Cut quality? Cut service? Buy cheaper? Increase productivity? What? You have to find the filler—piece by piece, dollar by dollar—to close up that gap, or you will have to admit that your earnings-growth objective was a pipe dream. If you feel that you must have the earnings growth, then you will have to chop out some of your development spending. That probably means sacrificing some sales growth, at least in the later years of the plan, and certainly revising some of your development objectives.

In the happy event that you have a negative planning gap in earnings—that is, your profit projection falls above your objective line—you can begin to pick over some of those projects in the idea bank, the ones that developed out of strengths and opportunities. If you really believe the profit projections, you can afford some additional investment spending in new developments, which will lift that curve out in the fourth and fifth year and beyond.

If you can get that earning projection back on the objective line, do you still have a gap in your profitability objective? Probably. Now the only cure left is to cut investment. Beware of proposals to lease assets. The after-tax rent will come right out of your earnings, which may give you a problem. But more significantly, it is a phony. It doesn't really change the total assets utilized. It is merely a way of financing them without having it show up on the balance sheet. It could be the cheapest way to borrow money, but it usually is not.

What you are really looking for is a way of turning over your capital faster. In current assets that means lower inventories, fewer receivables, smaller cash accounts. In fixed assets it means getting more sales out of a given physical facility. What specific programs can you think of to accomplish that sort of thing? The well-known Du Pont chart (Figure 11) is designed to emphasize this relationship of profitability to turnover. Maybe it will give you some ideas.

Hopefully, you will figure out enough believable programs to fill that gap and reach your objective rate of profitability. If you can't, then you have to decide whether you cut into the meat of your planned programs or accept a lower profitability objective. You make the choice, but you do have to choose. If you can't think of specific ways to increase that rate of return, there just are not enough good fairies wandering around to hand it to you for "trying harder."

Figure II. Relationship of factors affecting return on invested capital. (Courtesy of Du Pont)

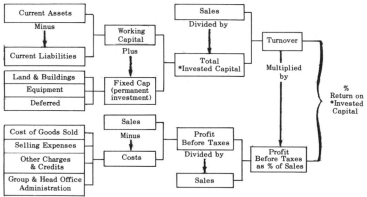

Equal to stockholders equity plus any long-term debt.

Once you come to terms with your profitability objective, you can turn everybody loose to work out the details of his or her part of the plan. That means essentially breaking the objectives down into successively smaller components until they are in working packages that one person or one group can accomplish in a finite time period for a predetermined cost.

SUGGESTED READING

Anonymous, "The Way I Make My Numbers Is for You Guys to Make Your Numbers," *Forbes* (February 15, 1972).

President David Mahoney, CEO of Norton Simon, Inc., tells how to achieve objectives.

Hughes, C. L., *Goal Setting* (AMACOM, 1965).

A psychologist's perspective on the segmenting of objectives in order to provide meaningful, operable goals for each level of management.

Kastens, M. L., "Whatever Happened to Plant Managers?" *Management Today* (August 1973).

Some observations about why production managers do not get involved in strategic decisions and why they should.

Kottler, J. L., "The Learning Curve: A Case History of Its Application," *Journal of Industrial Engineering*, Vol. 15, No. 4 (July–August 1964), pp. 176–180.

Discusses the learning-curve theory, which says that man-hours used per unit of production will decline by a constant percentage with each doubling of the total units that have been produced. This theory has been extended to apply to production costs other than labor.

Skinner, W., "Manufacturing—Missing Link in Corporate Strategy," *Harvard Business Review*, Vol. 47, No. 3 (May–June 1969).

A good article from the very skimpy literature on integrating manufacturing into corporate strategy.

Steiner, G. A., *Top Management Planning.* New York: The Macmillan Company, 1969, chap. 6.

The relationships of objectives and subobjectives.

9
The Hierarchy
of Objectives

The crucial question is: "What comes first?" rather than "What should be done?" . . . The normal human reaction is to evade the priority decision by doing a little bit of everything.
PETER DRUCKER

LET'S go back to the marketing plan. Let's assume that it was organized by product groups, with a special section on new products. All the product groups taken together plus a contribution from new products are planned to give you an increase in sales averaging 15 percent a year. Product group A is currently one of your hotter items and is believed to have potential for 25 percent growth in the first year, tapering off to 15 percent growth in the fifth year. Product group B has a different growth curve, as do C and D, and E and F. Improved products and line extensions are included in the performance of the different groups.

You are also counting on new sales contributions from products inherently different from those you are now marketing. Sales of these products are more problematical, but you must have them if you are going to make your 15 percent growth rate. Realistically, you know that you cannot count on a 100 percent batting average on new products. There will be delays in test market, recycling through the labs, start-up problems in production. This part of the marketing plan must play the odds. It must provide for the development of more new products than you need because some of them will bomb out. It must allow for reasonable slippage in product introduction, based on past experience. The new product development program must be run in such a way that, even given all the frailties to which new products are heir, you can in fact count on the sales contribution that you have built into your plan. If you can't afford a new product program at that level, don't plan on the new product sales.

Subobjectives

There are in fact six or seven subobjectives under the sales-growth primary objective. You know that if each of these subobjectives is achieved, the primary objective will be achieved automatically. You know further that if any of the subobjectives is missed, it is most unlikely that the primary objective will be achieved. This is the "necessary and sufficient rule." At any level in the hierarchy of objectives the sum of the subobjectives must be *sufficient* to automatically achieve the next higher objective. If any of the subobjectives could be missed without impairing the next higher objective, drop it out. It is *not necessary.*

You must accept direct responsibility for achieving the primary sales objective. However, you will designate some individual, some individual who reports directly to you, to be responsible for each of the subobjectives. Depending on how you are organized, you may designate all the sales subobjectives as the responsibility of one person. On the other hand, each may fall to the cognizance of different divisional general managers.

In any case, the individual selected must agree that the subobjective is reasonable and attainable. He or she may have suggested the objective in the first place, in which case there is no problem. But in delegating planning objectives, you must negotiate between what the lawyers call a "willing buyer and a willing seller." You can impose an objective on a subordinate. It's not hard. But you are most likely to end up with a collection of plausible excuses when the results are due rather than the performance you expected. Even if you break down the alibis, all you get is a moral victory—not results. You're better off to accept an objective that the subordinate is "sure" he or she can attain, and then hold his or her feet to the fire: No excuses! This is not "soft" management. It just keeps you from living temporarily in a fool's paradise.

If as a consequence of these negotiations the sum of your subobjectives does not add up to your primary objective, then you are on the spot. You ain't going to make it unless you change some part of the strategy, come up with some new ideas, some additional subobjectives to fill the gap. Crash the development program so the new products come out sooner. Improve the product even more. Change the pricing policy. Go into a new geographical area. Put more effort behind expanding your export sales. Produce some product for private label. Or somehow, some other way, bring a new dimension into the business.

If you can think of no practical options such as these, then you simply have to change the overall objective. If you can't really see any orderly way in which you can achieve the objective, no fairy godmother is going to make it happen for you. If 15 percent growth is just not in the cards, you may as well find it out now as several years from now. Scale down your ambitions or change the thrust of your business.

Let us assume that you will hold the sales vice-president responsible for the various product group objectives and the manager of product development responsible for the new product performance. They must realize that they are committed to the fulfillment of the objective, not merely the execution of the program that it is hoped will reach this objective. They get paid for accommodating unforeseen circumstances and changing their tactics to a more promising direction when they realize they are pursuing a fruitless task. You will hold them responsible for the results, and will consult with them on the means.

Discuss with each person how he or she expects to achieve his or her objective to assure that his or her ideas are realistic. Find out how the sales manager intends to segment his or her responsibility into the next level of subobjectives. Make suggestions. If during the planning period the manager decides to reshuffle the subobjectives, you should expect to be advised and have an opportunity to comment and approve. But keep it clearly understood that the essence of the contract is the result, not a series of actions. Don't set yourself up for the excuse, "Well, I did everything that we agreed I would do, but the sales just didn't come in." You never agreed on "everything the person would do." All you agreed on was the results he or she would achieve.

If you try to predetermine detailed courses of action, you take all the operational flexibility out of your organization. Furthermore, you take back the responsibility for the results because the implication is that if the course of action is followed competently, the results will follow. If they don't follow, the subordinate is off the hook.

So in delegating a subobjective, keep focused on the results and *insist* that the delegee retain tactical flexibility to achieve those results in the most expeditious manner possible.

Remember, the name of the game is, "You make your numbers and I'll make my numbers." If your subordinates make all their subobjectives and you have analyzed the requirements correctly, then you will make your objective. You really don't care how they achieved their objectives as long as the method was legal and did not jeopardize any other part of the objective network.

Sub-Subobjectives

The responsible subordinate will break down the subobjectives into further sub-subobjectives, which reflect his or her perception of how best to get the job done. As an example, let's take that first subobjective, which is the sales objective for product group A and is the responsibility of the sales vice-president. The way in which the vice-president breaks down this objective to the still lower level of subobjectives will depend to a substantial degree on how the sales department is organized.

If the department is organized geographically and has regional sales managers as well as an export manager, he or she will want to meet with each of these managers to discuss the potential for product group A sales in the individual's region over the next several years. He or she will tell the regional sales manager about the product improvement and line extensions that have been provided for in the marketing plan. He or she will show them the price forecast that has been used in the marketing plan. He or she will then ask each of them to set objectives by year in four categories:

1. Sales of present products to existing customers. This is essentially a baseline sales forecast.
2. Sales of present products to new customers in markets presently served, largely taken away from competition.
3. Sales to new customers, or even old customers, for applications in which the products are not presently used.
4. Sales of new products that are scheduled to be added to group A during the planning period.

If the sales vice-president is convinced that the regional manager's objectives are reasonable—neither irresponsibly high nor lackadaisically low—he or she figuratively signs a performance contract with the manager. The regional manager contracts to produce this kind of sales performance, on the condition that the corporation does provide the product improvements and line extensions promised, and does provide the new products on schedule. The regional manager may very well be reluctant to make this kind of commitment until he or she has consulted with the field sales force, in which case provisional figures are recorded subject to his or her confirmation or modification at a fixed date in the future.

The sales vice-president will then proceed to similar discussion of product group B, product group C, and so on with each of the regional managers.

Whether each regional manager makes an immediate or a deferred commitment, he or she will want to plan the hierarchy of objectives at another level with his or her subordinates. If he or she has district sales managers, he or she will consult with them in a manner analogous to the discussions that he or she has just had with the sales vice-president. District managers will in turn ultimately want to obtain the commitments of their individual sales people. If, on the other hand, the regional manager's area is organized by product rather than territory, he or she will have to rotate the matrix by 90 degrees and deal separately with the sales manager of each product.

The "Negotiated" Objective

At every level of the hierarchy the principle of the "negotiated" objective between a willing buyer and a willing seller prevails. If at any level the sum of the commitments obtained is not sufficient to meet the next higher-level objective, the responsible executive is obligated to try to devise some additional strategies to fill the gap. If the executive cannot—either because of a dearth of ideas or lack of adequate resources—he or she must go back to his or her superior and renegotiate the commitment. Then the superior has got to pick up the gap. Hopefully someone will have a productive idea before the problem is bucked all the way up to the level of primary objectives.

Thus you have a homeostatic system in which minor adjustments in strategy can be made as far down in the organization as the necessary resources are available. On the other hand, really serious hang-ups are automatically propagated up through the system and demand basic changes in the overall plan, rather than remaining submerged until they show up as missed objectives at the end of the planning period.

Segmenting sales objectives is a relatively simple job because the subobjectives are directly additive. Other kinds of objectives are more complicated because the tasks are multifaceted and it is seldom superficially apparent whether or not the several subobjectives will in fact add up to the superobjective. It takes the highest kind of management skill to identify, define, and assign the various component jobs that must be done to achieve a desired result. Not only is there often more than one way that the job can be approached, but—even given a single approach—there are often alternative ways in which subobjectives can be structured.

The marketing vice-president who has accepted the responsibility for sales of new products has several ways to break down that objective into manageable subobjectives. The simplest way would be to break it down into individual product projects. However, this is apt to be awkward and confusing in the far-out years unless the vice-president is dealing with very long lead-time products. He or she will probably find it more operationally convenient to approach the problem with subobjectives in the form: "Have a national rollout of at least two new products each year," or "Every year introduce to full market test new products having an annual sales potential of at least $500,000." Then if the vice-president uses each year as a separate subobjective, he or she will find that by using his or her lead-time experience, he or she can break down the job further into specific objectives in market research, product design, field testing, production engineering, market testing, distribution, and so forth, with discrete due dates for each and with individual responsibilities assigned.

Then if somebody somewhere down the line objects that it is impossible to predict what new products will be introduced to the market four or five years hence, the vice-president is perfectly justified in saying, "Yes, I know, but as long as the corporation is supporting a product development program, it is not unreasonable to expect a certain level of results without knowing all the details years in advance." The point is that you can plan to move along at a certain pace without knowing exactly where you are going to put your foot down for every step.

In the case of developmental objectives, the subobjectives

may be sequential. In other words, you may only be able to sketch in the ultimate subobjective and concentrate your immediate attention on completing the first step of attaining some intermediate objective, with the thought that the next step can be planned more effectively at that stage.

Take each of your primary objectives—both the "Big Three" (Chapter 4) and the development objectives—and go through the same process. Negotiate with one of your direct subordinates to accept responsibility for each subobjective. Be sure that you agree with the strategy whereby the subobjective has been broken down into sub-subobjectives. Then let your subordinate cascade the hierarchy of objectives down to the ultimate action level.

In describing the process of cascading objectives down through a hierarchy, one can't avoid making it sound more simple than it is. In the first place, the process is not so linear as it sounds; it doesn't go all in one direction, from the top down. In the example we have been using, there presumably was a considerable up-flow of information during the preparation of the strategic marketing plan. The generation of that information would have in large measure anticipated the eventual "negotiation" of subobjectives. The normal sequence is: The information flows up the organization to where the high-level objectives are set. Then the discussions move down the organization until they get to the point at which the work will actually be done. Finally, the details of a myriad of individual action plans are aggregated and passed back up the hierarchy to see whether they all hang together and still add up to the attainment of the primary objectives.

Very often, when the information arrives at the top, it doesn't add up to the grand hopes of the policy-level officers. The job just can't be done, or at least not that fast or at a tolerable cost. Well, better to find it out now than later. Sometimes additional strategies or resources can be introduced to get things back on the desired track. If not, at least there is an opportunity to consider priorities and consciously allocate resources to the most important ends. Without this opportunity, too often the resources are spread around evenly, and all efforts end up half-starved. Alternatively, the situation may turn out to be first-come-first-served. Then the slower starting development project that really holds the key to the company's future will find the cupboard bare just when it needs support.

There is a sort of natural phenomenon that occurs in a company when it first starts formal planning. When the managers establish an orderly, structured procedure for considering the needs and potentialities of their enterprise, they suddenly find so many things that must, should, or might be done —things they probably would not have thought of otherwise— that they can't begin to do them all. This usually happens in the third or fourth year of their planning effort because that is about the stage when the cyclic process is beginning to get up to speed. It can be a frustrating and perhaps a little frightening time.

What it means, though, is simply that for the first time the management has got some real choices. The executives responsible can decide what is more or less important and select from among real alternatives. They no longer are limited to reacting to whatever happens to land on their desks at the moment. They are finally getting some control over the destiny of the company. It can be a new and exciting experience.

But to get to that point, the hierarchical cycle must be completed. The plans have to be propagated all the way through the organization in ever increasing detail until they get to the working-project level. Only at that point can the actual resource cost be determined. Then these costs can be aggregated up along the line to see whether the total is supportable. If that cycle is not completed and the plan is left dangling from the top, its chances of fulfillment are not very good.

SUGGESTED READING

Granger, C. H., "The Hierarchy of Objectives," *Harvard Business Review*, Vol. 42, No. 3 (May–June 1974).

The classic discussion of segmenting objectives.

Humphrey, A. S., "Getting Management Commitment to Planning a New Approach," *Long Range Planning*, Vol. 7, No. 1 (February 1974).

Good tips on conducting group-planning sessions and propagating planning activity down through the organization. May underestimate the time required and overestimate the discipline possible.

Payne, B., *Planning for Company Growth*. New York: McGraw-Hill Book Company, 1963, chaps. 5, 8, and 10.

Good chapters on marketing plan, manufacturing plan, and financial plan.

Scott, B. W., *Long-Range Planning in American Industry*. (AMACOM, 1965), chap. 7.

Good chapter on planning assumptions.

Walker, E. H., and Baughn, W. H., *Financial Planning and Policy*. New York: Harper & Row, 1961.

Good basic text on financial planning.

10
Who's Going
to Do It?

Efficiency is doing things—not wishing you could do them, dreaming about them or wondering if you can do them.
FRANK CRANE

THE last step in the planned management of a company is to plan the individual action projects that will make the whole thing happen. This is in many respects the easiest part of the process, although it does take time. It is also the part of the process that is most frequently slighted or not completed, with the consequence that the grand plan never comes to fruition.

There is a lot of sophisticated literature on project planning. Project planning can be PERT-charted, computerized, designed with all sorts of homeostatic controls, and otherwise made very elegant. These techniques can be very powerful, especially when they are used on single-purpose projects that are very complex—like putting a man on the moon or even moving into a new office building. However, in a small business you can get most of the benefits of project planning by relatively primitive techniques that require no special training or unusual skill. Performance will improve considerably with practice, however. You can lay out project plans at any level of your hierarchy of objectives. If you do it at higher levels, it is often called "program planning."

Each responsible person in your hierarchy of objectives must have a procedure for monitoring progress against sub-objectives. The person should be able to assure himself or herself that the individual projects are moving forward acceptably, but he or she does not have to have detailed knowledge of exactly what is going on at every point in time if he or she is not directly supervising the ultimate action steps. The person can develop program plans in whatever detail suits his or her style. However, at the level of direct supervision, project or "action" plans are most important and should be done in considerable detail. This probably is the level of responsibility of your district sales manager, or your research team leader, or your chief accountant, or—in the case of production—probably your plant manager, not the foreperson.

Many people think of "project" plans in terms of discrete undertakings that have a beginning and an end—like building a plant or developing a new product. This does not have to be the case. You can "projectize" any task. All you have to do is put it in a time frame and put a finite objective at the end of it. Thus an existing sales force might set up a "project" to "increase sales in Region Two to the level of $1 million a month by January 1977." A production department might set out to "reduce the reject rate to one percent of completed units by July of 1976." Then the responsible manager can decide everything that has to be done, by when and by whom, in order to attain that objective. And the manager can calculate how much it will cost. A project plan is a very powerful tool and much superior to merely resolving to "concentrate sales effort in Region Two" or to "aggressively strive to reduce reject rate to an acceptable level."

The Action Sequence

The trick in project management is simply to sit back and visualize how a series of actions will progress before you ever start them. This takes some imagination, and that is why some people find it difficult to do. However, anybody worthy of managerial responsibility at any level can attain a working grasp of the technique with a little practice.

The first step is to merely take a yellow pad and start listing all the things that are going to have to be done to complete the project and attain the established objective. List them in approximate chronological order. This is not like an appointment book that says what is going to happen every day or every hour, but rather is a listing by title of the various definable tasks that will have to be completed. To a certain extent, the degree of detail will reflect the personality of the project leader and also his or her style in assigning responsibility.

Next to each action task put an estimate of the number of man-hours or man-days or man-weeks, depending on the scope of the project, which you think will be required to accomplish that phase.

At this stage consider only the key category of personnel involved: engineers, trainers, market researchers, and so on. We will refine the estimates later. What you want here is only an early warning if you are overcommitting your personnel resources and thus underestimating elapsed time. Now in a second column, taking into account what you know of the workload of the people who will have to do the job, what is a reasonable estimate of the elapsed time that must be allowed for the action to be completed? Allow time for the routine duties of the individuals as well as for meetings, minor crises, sick leave, and all other activities that will delay the project. If approvals and consultations are involved, be sure to allow some slippage for preparing documents, trying to get in touch with somebody who is out of town, delays in calling meetings, and all the other frustrations of organizational life.

Now you can begin to spread out your action steps along a time line. Start from today or the day of project initiation. Follow your initial conception of how the project should progress. Put down what you think must be started first and then what can be started when the first task is completed, and then the next step, and the next. Some phases may be nonsequential and can parallel the main sequence. These should be coordinated with the main sequence, entering their due dates at the point where the results will be required, and then calculating back to determine the latest possible starting date. A simple Gantt chart is helpful at this point if you want to get that complicated.

The series of sequentially dependent steps will give you a kind of primitive "critical path." The sum of the elapsed-time estimates for this series indicates the total project time. If this time exceeds the target date for the objective, go back over the series and see whether any of the steps can be telescoped to save elapsed time.

Do not delude yourself by thinking that you can compress the time schedule by making people work harder. Unless you have a very slack organization, people are working about as hard as they can and there just isn't that much slack to be taken up. It is possible that elapsed time can be shortened by scheduling overtime or by putting more personnel on the job, either on loan from other activities or through the use of outside services. If you cannot get the cumulative elapsed time down to fit the objective due date, you'd better tell somebody about it now and see whether you can get the due date changed.

In some cases there may be no point in doing the project at all if it's going to take "that long." In other cases other parts of the organization may be counting on the completion of your plan to coincide with work they may be doing or planning to do subsequently. It's useless for them to break their backs if your project is going to come in substantially after the scheduled date. It is always hard to tell the boss that you really cannot finish the job in the time, or to the degree, or at the cost that he or she would like. However, if this is in fact the case, the boss is going to find out at the end of the job anyhow. It is a lot easier to explain it at the beginning rather than after the schedule has been missed and the budget overspent, and he or she is in a state of frustration, disillusionment, and sometimes outright rage.

Once you get your project scheduled, before you do anything else you should talk to the various people involved in the separate action steps. Be sure their schedules concur with both the estimates of personnel requirements and the allowed time estimates at the time or by the due date that you have scheduled for their participation. This consultation should involve not only your subordinates but also, and particularly, staff departments or other parallel organization groups that must contribute to the successful completion of the project. Such people know a good deal more about their commitments than you do. If they are not going to perform for you on schedule, it is better for you to find out now and try to provide for it than to get into a flap in the middle of the project because somebody "let you down."

The Project Summary

Once you get everybody checked out on the project as you see it, you can start to make up a project summary (see Figure 12). It need not be complicated. Put the statement of the objective at the top, followed by a short paragraph describing the project, your general approach to it, and any underlying assumptions involved in the design of the project. Now list your action steps in the order of their completion dates. You have probably added some steps to your original list. You can put the beginning dates over on the extreme left-hand side if you want. Immediately to the right of the description of the action step, put the due date.

In a column to the right of the due date, put the name of the individual responsible for completing the action. Do not put the name of a department in this column. If you are dealing through the department head, put his or her name there. If you know who is actually doing the work, put that person's name there. The sequence of due dates already gives you a crude control mechanism. You can run down that column to the current date every Monday morning—or every morning, if you want—and see just where you are in trouble.

Now, when you set up this project plan, by implication

Figure 12. Action project summary.

Objective:		Project Manager:	
Description:		Approved: ___ Total Expense $ _____	Target Date: ___ Total Investment $ _____
Assumptions: 1. 2. 3.		4. 5.	

Start Date	Action Steps	Due Date	Respon-sibility	Review/ Approval Dates	Decision Dates

you assumed that everything was going to go along pretty much as you originally conceived it. Still, you know that that is very unlikely to be the case. So make a third column for review/approval dates. You will probably want to key these with some kind of code. For example: (1) periodic (monthly) review with project team, (2) review and go ahead with department head, (3) review with steering committee, (4) approval by vice-president required to proceed.

You will need one more column to indicate decision dates. It is a good psychological trick to draw a heavy line across this sheet wherever you have a decision date. It is usually not worthwhile to detail all the branches of the decision tree—that is, to make alternative plans for each possibility beyond the points of decision. Schedule what you think will be the most likely course of development; and then if ultimately you have to scrap that plan and redesign it, so be it.

Decision Criteria

However, what is worth doing is to set down your decision criteria at the beginning of the project rather than on the decision date. It is much easier to get agreement on such criteria in the relatively cool-headed atmosphere of project planning than it is midway through the project when people begin to have emotional and conceivably political investments in the project.

If there is going to be a market-study phase, get agreement in advance of the characteristics of the market that will be acceptable to warrant continuation of the project. If there is going to be prototype-design phase, get down in writing the performance levels that will have to be achieved by the proto-type to justify proceeding into production engineering. If there is going to be a test of a new information system, what level of output from the system will justify installing it throughout the organization?

These decision criteria can be referenced in an appendix to the project summary. It is wise to also include in another appendix the names of the people who will be involved in making the decision as to whether to proceed with the project, abort it, or redesign it.

There is one other item you will want on your project progress summary sheet (see Figure 13). It can be set up on the back of the schedule forms or on a separate sheet. This is a resource allocation schedule that summarizes by months over the life of the project the man-days allocated to the project, broken down into managerial, professional, and clerical cate-gories. You can break it down finer if you want. It also shows the rate of expenditure by month, separated into capital and expense items.

Your original rough estimates of manpower requirements will give you a start on this personnel allocation summary. By the time you get to the end of the form, you will have a much more exact idea of what is going to be involved. The expenditure summary is essentially an abstract of your project budget, which presumably you prepared for somebody.

These resource allocation summaries can be used for

Figure 13. Resource allocation schedule.

Month	Manpower (MD)			Money	
	Managerial	Professional	Clerical	Expense	Capital
Total					

several purposes. They can be added up through the objective tree to any level desired to determine how much money and effort is being expended against a given objective. The personnel allocation can be converted into imputed cost by using cost-per-day factors for the various levels of personnel, and a formal cost/benefit analysis can be undertaken. Even if such an analysis is not done formally, it is very easy to make an intuitive judgment as to whether the level of effort is commensurate with the importance of the objective. There can be misallocations, both over or under the optimal.

The rate of expenditure profile is of course useful to the controller in estimating cash flow needs and, in the extreme case, in enabling him or her to blow the whistle if there are more action projects than the company can afford.

Underperformance or Overcommitment

Actually, shortage of money is less likely to be a problem than overcommitment of the personnel resources. One of the hazards of the project approach to management tasks is that it involves consideration of personnel or organizational commitments in vertical slices. You look at problems project by project and tend to say, "Yes, we could do that. We could get it done by such and such a date." If there isn't a mechanism for adding the commitment across horizontally, there is great risk that the sum of the individual project commitments will grossly exceed the personnel resources available. This can happen in specialized support groups, although such people are often accustomed to organizing their work on a project basis and have some kind of scheduling board or other mechanism for avoiding such overcommitment.

In a sales department, however, or in a plant maintenance group, for instance—where there is a lot of repetitive routine activity—the individuals tend to be "good soldiers" and agree to take on special tasks on a "we can fit it in somehow" basis. You can fit in only so much. If there is any single prevailing reason why plans do not get implemented or do not get implemented on time, it isn't underperformance but overcommitment. The resources just were not available to do the job, and frequently there is no way that they could have been obtained. You have to provide every procedural crutch you can conceive of to protect yourself against this hypercooperative overcommitment. If you do not, you will too frequently find yourself entertaining foolish hopes that projects will get done even though they never had a chance from the beginning.

There is likely to be some resistance from supervisory management people if they are asked to prepare action project plans. You can tell them it is good management training in analyzing and scheduling their tasks, which will become increasingly important as their responsibilities increase. It is, but they may not be impressed. You can tell them it will keep them out of trouble by preventing them from promising things that they cannot deliver. They may not believe you. You can explain that it will help keep their people happier by avoiding crash assignments and deadline crises. They may *like* it a little hectic—"Keeps people on their toes."

If they have never done action project planning, it sounds

a little forbidding, rigid, overorganized. What they will tell you is: "It takes too much time." It really doesn't have to, and the odds are that it will save ten times as much time by eliminating lost motion. But keep it simple: a minimum of forms and procedures. Actually, after a little practice, the "yellow sheet" project outline for most projects can be done in less than an hour.

What takes the most time is checking out the various people who will have to contribute to the project to see whether they will agree to the schedule. In some way this would have to be done anyhow, but without a plan it might be done too late or so informally that there is no mutual appreciation of the commitment. That's how good ideas get fouled up, people get mad, and the alibis begin. Making up a project summary as a control device takes a little time, but not too much after all the information is available.

One thing that should be strongly emphasized to the project leader is that the action project plan is his or her management tool. Once the boss has gone over it with him or her, approved it, and abstracted the resource allocation data, the boss is not going to follow all the steps in the plan. He or she will keep a copy for the record but is not likely to look at it much unless something goes badly awry. The project leader has to live with the plan; and if the individual does use it as a continuous management tool, life will be much easier.

Combining Action Plans and Budgets

As the action project plans are completed, they will be reviewed and aggregated at the next level of management. Inevitably, they will be much more detailed for the upcoming year than for the years further along in the planning period. Thus this review and assembly of long-range projects can and should be combined with the annual budget preparation.

This procedure has several virtues. It assures not only that the detailed first year of the long-range plan and the next year's budget are consistent but also that they are practically synonymous. The significant long-term efforts have a chance to get factored into the operating budget on something like an equal footing with the ongoing activities. And management at all levels gets a chance to look at the total disposition of resources at one time.

As the numbers work their way back up the hierarchy, there will be some considerable cutting and fitting and shuffling of effort at all management levels. This is all to the good. These trade-offs should be made at this time and at these levels if at all possible. When the project planning was initiated, the strategic objective structure had already been accepted in principle. Hopefully, there will be enough imagination and accommodation in the organization so that by the time the totals get back up to the executive levels, the major strategic objectives will have survived essentially intact.

If they haven't, the people in top management have only two choices: (1) accept more modest strategic objectives, at least for the present, and hope for some smarter ideas as they go through the planning cycle again next year or (2) start digging down through the details of the action programs, looking for the weak member that is stalling the forward thrust of the enterprise. If they choose the second course and they do find the clinker, they may find that they cannot do much to get the situation shored up within the next year and will have to live with more modest results, at least through that year anyhow.

The End and the Beginning

As a consequence, the final planning meeting of the cycle is apt to be as much a stock-taking session as anything else. If the objective commitments have held up through the completion of the planning, it is a time for mutual congratulations. If they have not, it is a time to resolve to do better next time.

About the only substantive thing to be done is to schedule the first planning session for the next year—because you never get done with this damn planning job! As long as you keep getting smarter, you will keep making new plans. If your plans don't change from year to year, it is a sure sign that you are not learning anything.

Start by requesting a new market analysis, just as you said you would last year, and go through the same cycle of steps. Don't try to short-circuit any of them because the time schedule is self-correcting. If everyone is happy with your definition of the corporate mission and the established strategic policies, you won't have to spend much time on them. But take an hour or two once a year just to confirm that everyone is still playing in the same ball game. If the discussions begin to stretch out, either you have some "talkers" in your group—and by now you ought to know who they are and how to shut them up—or there is some real uncertainty about the proper posture of the firm. In the latter case, you had better take the time, get the questions out on the table, and thrash out a new consensus.

As you go around the planning cycle again, you will know better how much time to allow for the various phases. Some things will go much faster as you gain experience. However, you are also likely to find that as you gain time through increased skill, you will reinvest it in more sophisticated analyses and more far-ranging speculation about opportunities.

There is one place you will save a lot of time in the second round if you stick to your guns in the first round. Insist that people do their homework. Refuse to accept a bunch of numbers cobbled up the night before the meeting. Don't spend your time listening to a lot of glib generalizations and blue-sky hopes and dreams. You have to convince people that planning sessions are not old-fashioned "review and forecast" meetings, where a plausible story and a couple of fancy graphs will get by. What you need are rigorous arguments with a credible explanation for events in the past and hard reasons for every expectation of the future.

Most people won't believe you when you tell them that is what is required—probably because it's hard work and they may not know how to do it. The only way to make believers out of them is to keep sending them back to the drawing board until they come up with a passable product. They'll learn, and you won't waste a lot of time wading through a verbal fog trying to find the germ of an idea. Furthermore, you won't waste everybody's time and enthusiasm by drawing up a bunch of plans based on questionable assumptions and unsupportable hypothese that just never are going to work out.

Of course even the best of plans are not self-propelled. They have to be "worked." You need a control system to assure that, *in fact,* events are proceeding "according to plan." Planning and control are two sides of the same coin. The plan makes it possible to control the progress of your enterprise. The corresponding control system assures that progress does occur. One without the other is apt to be an idle exercise.

SUGGESTED READING

Buffa, E. S., *Modern Production Management.* New York: John Wiley & Sons, 1965.

Includes an excellent overview of various scheduling devices and systems available. Does not have to be limited to production management.

Fertakis, J., and Moss, J., "An Introduction to PERT and PERT/Cost Systems," *Managerial Planning* (January–February 1971).

An easy, nontechnical introduction to PERT techniques.

Jerome, W. T., *Executive Control: The Catalyst.* New York: John Wiley & Sons, 1961, pp. 90–114.

A good treatment of the relationship between planning and budgeting.

Martino, R. L., *Project Management and Control* (AMACOM, 1965), three volumes.

The three volumes together provide a relatively unsophisticated system for analyzing and scheduling projects. The third volume gets pretty complicated, but if you have complicated projects, it is worth reading. Uses PERT/CPM and a resource allocation routine.

Novick, D., "Long-Range Planning Through Program Budgeting," *Business Horizons* (February 1969).

Basic introduction to the Planning-Programming-Budgeting (PPB) system originated in the U.S. Defense Department and subsequently extended widely throughout the federal government.

Starr, M. K., *Management: A Modern Approach.* New York: Harcourt Brace Jovanovich, Inc., 1971, chap. 9.

A representative discussion of the more sophisticated forms of project planning.

Steiner, G. A., and Ryan, W. G., *Industrial Project Management.* New York: Crowell Collier and Macmillan, Inc., 1968.

One of the few books on project management that is not totally biased to the defense/aerospace complex.

11
Make It Happen

If anything can go wrong—it will.
MURPHY

THERE is some very simple arithmetic that should guide you in setting up a system for working your plan. You will probably have between four and eight strategic objectives for which you are directly and ultimately responsible—that is, objectives you have to achieve because if you don't, nobody else will. If you are the chief executive officer, these are the primary objectives of the company. If you accept direct personal responsibility for as many as ten objectives, you may be in trouble, for reasons that will become apparent shortly. For this example, we will assume that you have five objectives to worry about.

Say you have taken each of your objectives and broken it down into subobjectives and, after suitable negotiation, have delegated each one to a subordinate. Your business judgment tells you that these subobjectives can be accomplished with the resources available to you and that, if they are accomplished, you will make your objective. If you can keep all those subobjectives on the track, you will have your plan under control and will be moving the company where you want it to go.

Presumably the individual responsible for each of the subobjectives reports directly to you, so you should be able to exercise full accountability. If he or she doesn't, probably you should reconsider your organizational setup.

The Point of Control

These subobjectives are your level of control. You will want to monitor progress against them monthly to be sure you understand what is going on in these dimensions and why there are deviations from plan projections. In order to do that, you need reliable data on performance for each of these subobjectives. If your management information system does not provide you with such data, fix up the management information system. That's what an MIS is for—to keep the management informed of what is going on in critical areas of the business. You have defined the critical areas by the way in which you structured your objectives. You may find that when you get the entire objective structure worked out, the MIS is retrieving a lot of data that does not relate to anybody's objectives. In that case those data are probably not of much use, and you can consider pruning the data processing routines.

Now, when you delegate the subobjectives, you are certainly not going to simply lay them on the table and assume that your subordinate will get them done somehow. You need to know how the individual is going to go about it, and want to be sure that you think his or her tactics are do-able. He or she is going to break the responsibilities down into a series of tactical programs, and set an objective and assign responsibility for each program. This step gives him or her the set of subobjectives that become his or her points of control.

You will want to review and approve these programs and objectives before you tell the subordinate to go ahead. You are not going to try to control progress against any of these individual programs. That's your subordinate's job. You don't want to undercut or override his or her authority and thereby dilute his or her responsibility—and anyhow you couldn't do it. This is where the arithmetic comes in.

We said you had five primary objectives. Let's assume, modestly, that you broke each one of those down into five subobjectives. That gives you 25 points of control that you are going to manage closely. If each of those subobjectives is further subdivided into five tactical programs, that's 125 programs. If you tried to review that many programs in one day a month, you couldn't spend as many as five minutes on each of them. That's not control. That's kidding yourself.

You can, however, evaluate the conceptual soundness and practical reasonableness of 125 programs once a year. That's where you make your contribution and, if necessary, exercise veto power. That's where you find out 'how your subordinate perceives his or her job, because what are *tactical programs* to you constitute his or her *strategy* in pursuing objectives.

It also should be apparent that if you have a "flatter" organization, in which you accept personal responsibility for ten primary objectives that are then subdivided into ten subobjectives and so on, the numbers quickly get out of control. Ten times ten is 100 points of control, and times ten again would give you 1,000 tactical programs.

The moral of this little arithmetic exercise is: You have a level of *direct responsibility*. You *control* at the next level of detail. You *approve* at the next level of greater detail. And that's about all you can handle responsibly.

The Planning Books

With these principles in mind, it is pretty easy to design a planning book. Since your plans are not going to be static, you have your planning sheets in a loose-leaf binder. Everybody should be kept continuously aware of the basic rules of the game: The first page in the book is the statement of company mission, and the second page is the statement of estab-

lished strategic policies. Next come the *primary objectives* of
the company, since everybody should know where the company thinks it's going (see Figure 14). At the top of the primary objective sheet is an overall general strategy statement,
two or three sentences stating broadly what will be the guid-
ing principles in the development of the enterprise during the
planning period. Each of the primary objectives is stated in
text and then in numbers, if possible, along with an appropriate historical series.

In general, if you are making a five-year plan, you should
show a five-year history plus current year estimated. If it is a
ten-year plan, show a ten-year history. If you are graphically
oriented, you can add a page on which the history and objective lines are all shown in small line graphs. If all the lines
dogleg sharply in a positive direction, starting next year, you
are probably living in a dream world.

Finally, on the bottom section of the page list basic assumptions that underlie all the judgments in the plan (we will
run in some more detailed assumptions later). In most cases
these would include assumptions on inflation rate, cost of
money, possibly the population growth in some industries,
government regulations—in general, the "all bets are off" kind
of potentialities.

Now let's be honest. Nobody is going to read the front
pages of your planning book very often, but they should be
there as a kind of nagging presence to keep reminding people
just what the company is all about.

Beyond these introductory pages, everybody's book is different. It is divided into two sections: *Direct Responsibility*
and *Control*. You may want to have a second binder for
backup material, of which more will be said later.

Direct Responsibility

In the direct-responsibility section, each manager has in
his or her book one sheet for every objective for which he or
she is personally responsible (see Figure 15). At the top of
the sheet is a statement of the objective, followed by the quan-

Figure 14. Strategic plan — 1975-1980: Primary objectives.

Primary Objectives

General Strategy

The planning period will be one of balanced growth in
sales and earnings and improved profitability. A major
effort will be directed to increasing overseas sales
and to correct an unsatisfactory supply situation.

	1970	1971	1972	1973	1974	1975	1976	1977	1978	1979	1980

I   Increase sales volume by an average of 15% per year.

($000,000)

1970	1971	1972	1973	1974	1975	1976	1977	1978	1979	1980
10.0	18.0	28.0	35.0	41.0	(47.0)	54.0	61.0	69.0	81.0	93.0

II   Increase earnings A/T by an average of 15% per year.

($000,000)

1970	1971	1972	1973	1974	1975	1976	1977	1978	1979	1980
-5.0	0.5	2.5	3.8	4.0	(4.5)	5.2	6.0	6.9	7.9	9.0

III   Achieve a minimum ROA of 12.5% A/T.

(percent)

1970	1971	1972	1973	1974	1975	1976	1977	1978	1979	1980
-20.0	1.9	8.0	8.1	8.5	(9.0)	9.5	10.0	11.3	12.5	12.5

IV   Increase overseas sales by 25% per year.

($000,000)

1970	1971	1972	1973	1974	1975	1976	1977	1978	1979	1980
-	-	2.0	2.5	3.0	(3.6)	4.5	5.5	7.0	9.0	11.0

V   Be in production of subcomponent "X" by 1978.

(units,000)

1970	1971	1972	1973	1974	1975	1976	1977	1978	1979	1980
-	-	-	-	-	-	-	10	50	55	60

Critical Assumptions

Price increases 4-6% per year.
Prime rate 10% or less after June 1975.
No equity financing.
No major technological obsolescence.
No new competitors.
Free access to Japanese market.

Figure I5. Strategic plan — 1975-1980: Breakdown of Objective I.

Sect: <u>Resp</u>. Sheet <u>I</u>
Approved <u>BDP</u> Date <u>6/7/75</u>
Resp. <u>C.E. Owen</u>

Objective I

<u>1970</u>	<u>1971</u>	<u>1972</u>	<u>1973</u>	<u>1974</u>	<u>1975</u>	<u>1976</u>	<u>1977</u>	<u>1978</u>	<u>1979</u>	<u>1980</u>

Increase sales volume by an average of 15% per year.

($000,000)

10.0	18.0	28.0	35.0	41.0	(47.0)	54.0	61.0	69.0	81.0	93.0

Strategy

The marketing strategy will be to hold OEM market share
in product groups "B" and "C" and pursue the after market
aggressively. Major growth is expected in product group
"A," particularly in the export market.

Sub-Objectives

<u>1970</u>	<u>1971</u>	<u>1972</u>	<u>1973</u>	<u>1974</u>	<u>1975</u>	<u>1976</u>	<u>1977</u>	<u>1978</u>	<u>1979</u>	<u>1980</u>

($000,000)

<u>I-A</u> Increase sales volume Group A by an average of 20% per year.
    --Responsible: R. Brown

-	-	2	4	6	(8)	10	12	14	17	20

<u>I-B</u> Increase sales volume Group B by an average of 9% per year.
    --Responsible: J. Jones

6	12	16	18	19	(21)	23	25	27	30	33

<u>I-C</u> Increase sales volume Group C by an average of 11% per year.
    --Responsible: B. Smith

4	6	10	13	16	(18)	20	22	24	27	30

<u>I-D</u> Introduce improved C-widget by 1976.
    --Responsible: M. Doe

-	-	-	-	-	-	1	5	10	12	13

<u>I-E</u> Achieve $10 M sales from new products by 1980.
    --Responsible: C.Seidel

-	-	-	-	-	-	1	2	4	7	10

Critical Assumptions

No destructive price competition in the market.
No Group B products are delisted by FDA.
Strip mining of western coal is allowed under reasonable
    environmental constraints.

tified history and future targets. Then there is a strategy statement outlining the general approach to the achievement of the objective. Then comes the list of subobjectives that have been agreed upon as necessary and sufficient to complete the top objective, along with quantified history and targets as appropriate.

Obviously a great deal of consonance must exist between the strategy statement and the list of subobjectives. The subobjectives, after all, are a detailing and quantification of the strategy, and in their totality must add up to the complete strategy. If this relationship is not clearly apparent, there is probably some muddy thinking involved somewhere.

The bottom of the form contains a list of critical assumptions on which both the chosen strategy and the specific objectives are premised.

You can have special forms printed up for these planning book sheets if you want to, but if you can discipline your people to use a standard format, a blank sheet will give you a little more flexibility.

You are going to need some kind of indexing system for the book and associated appendixes, and an identification system for files. One useful scheme is to use capital roman numerals for the primary objectives, capital letters for the first set of subobjectives, then arabic numbers, a lower-case letter, and more numbers as necessary. This gives a citation like

I, B, 3, c, 4

If that looks too forbidding, you can do it all in arabic numbers, something like this:

1: 2: 3: 3: 4

This system really is not so bad when you get used to it.

You should have an indexing code up in the upper right-hand corner of each sheet, which might look something like this:

Sect:	Control	Sheet: 1-A-2
Approved: G.W.		Date: 6/7/75
Resp.:	J. Jones	

The first sheets in the direct-responsibility section should be for objectives to correct weaknesses, those assigned to the manager whose book is involved, since these have the highest priority and hopefully can be removed fairly soon. These can be coded W-1, W-2, and so on. The CEO will have sheets corresponding to these objectives in his or her control section. Other special assignment objectives sheets will follow. The assignments in the regular hierarchy of objectives come last.

The totality of the direct-responsibility section constitutes the total responsibility of an individual for the future success of the company. If it is too much, the individual had better find out now—and scream. If he or she cannot do it, it is better to tell the boss now and take the immediate flak rather than fall on his or her face a year from now and get everyone in trouble. Most plans fail because people commit themselves to more than they can possibly do, not because they are stupid, lazy, incompetent, or malicious. It is the person who makes the assignments who is ultimately responsible for the overburdening commitments, and he or she is the one who will ultimately take the blame.

Control

In the control section of your planning book you will have one sheet for each subobjective for which you are indirectly responsible (see Figure 16). There will be about 25 of them. Each sheet will start with the objective and a "strategy" statement of the general approach to the problem. This will be followed by a list of program objectives that will be pursued to attain this subobjective. This sheet is a summary of the strategy and objectives that your subordinate proposed to you as means of achieving the objective for which he or she is directly responsible.

You approve the approach and the rate of progress expressed by the program objectives. But you will measure performance against your control-level subobjective and not attempt to monitor all the programs the subordinate has proposed.

Figure 16.   Strategic plan — 1975-1980: Breakdown of Subobjective I-B.

Sect: <u>Control</u> Sheet <u>I-B</u>
Approved <u>CEO</u> Date <u>6/7/75</u>
Resp. <u>J. Jones</u>

<u>Objective I-B</u>

<u>1970</u>	<u>1971</u>	<u>1972</u>	<u>1973</u>	<u>1974</u>	<u>1975</u>	<u>1976</u>	<u>1977</u>	<u>1978</u>	<u>1979</u>	<u>1980</u>

Increase sales volume Group B by an average of 9% per year.

($000,000)

6	12	16	18	19	(21)	23	25	27	30	33

<u>Strategy</u>

The OEM for "B's" appears to be flattening out and after
about the middle of the planning period our sales growth
other than price effect must come from the after market.
We cannot expect to improve our present 40% SOM substantially in the face of intensifying competition without a
technological breakthrough which we cannot foresee.

<u>Sub-Objectives</u>

<u>1970</u>	<u>1971</u>	<u>1972</u>	<u>1973</u>	<u>1974</u>	<u>1975</u>	<u>1976</u>	<u>1977</u>	<u>1978</u>	<u>1979</u>	<u>1980</u>

($000,000)

<u>1-B-1</u> Develop after market sales.
        --Responsible: M. Watt

-	-	-	-	-	-	0.2	0.5	1.0`	3.0	6.0

<u>1-B-2</u> Maintain 40% SOM of OEM.
        --Responsible: J. Ware

6	12	16	18	19	(21)	23	24.5	26	27	27

<u>Critical Assumptions</u>

No technological breakthrough by competition.
Price increases averaging 4% per year (less than general price
    inflation).
Continued increase in natural gas prices to at least
    $2.00/MCF by 1978.

The control sheet in your book will duplicate the direct-responsibility sheet in your subordinate's book. This gives the individual a sheet in his or her control section that details each program to the next level of responsibility, and he or she will monitor and control progress at that level.

You will want a control calendar for each of your control-level subobjectives (see Figure 17). This will be a chronological list of the critical events that must occur if the objective you are controlling is to be attained. Work out with your subordinate an agreed-upon schedule of due dates, reviews, approval points, and decision points for the programs the individual is supervising. It takes some judgment, skill, and a little imagination to make up one of these calendars. There are no arbitrary rules for setting milestones for a program, but you will get better at it with practice. Set up your control sheets as far into the future as you can reasonably see. You can replace them and augment them any time you want.

You should follow every control sheet with a one-page

Figure 17. Control calendar.

Subobjective I-B: Increase sales volume of Group B by an average of 9% per year.				
Due Date	*Resp.*	*Milestones*	*Action Required*	*By Whom*
2/01/76	J. W.	Submit plan for reorganization of distribution department and system.	Approval Concurrence	CEO Product. Mgr.
2/10/76	B. R.	Budget for development of improved fragel valve.	Concurrence Concurrence	CEO Financial Off.
3/01/76	M. W.	Copy and layout for customer service manual due.	None	
3/01/76	M. W.	Proposal for consumer promotion campaign	Approval Concurrence	CEO Financial Off.
4/10/76 . . etc..	J. J.	First quarter sales review.	Review	Exec. Comm.

graphical presentation of month-to-month performance of each subobjective against target. It does not require much work; you do not have to redraw the charts; just have your secretary draw in the latest monthly data as they become available. For most people it is easier to spot a divergence in a graph line than in a table of numbers. Of course if you spot an aberration and do not do anything about it, nobody can help you.

You will probably want to "flag" each one of your control sheets with a special index tab because these are what you will be working from continually. You (or your secretary, if you have a good one) should check them every Monday morning. I know this is a long-range plan, but if you don't stay on top of it all the time, there ain't going to be no long range. You don't have to check with your subordinate every week. You don't even have to talk with him or her every month if the individual is producing according to plan unless he or she asks to talk to you. You spend your time on the person who is *not* producing up to commitments.

Your subordinate, of course, will have individual control sheets on each of the programs listed under your control-level subobjectives and will be riding herd on performance against those objectives. That's what that person gets paid for. When you get far enough down the hierarchy to the point that someone is actively supervising an action program, the control sheet becomes identical with the project action plan.

Summary of Responsibility

The last section in your book is a *summary* (see Figure 18). This is a personal summation of your planned responsibilities and commitments. Of course, for the CEO it will be the summary for the whole enterprise.

Down the left side you list the objectives for which you are personally responsible. Under each responsibility-level objective, list each of the related control-level subobjectives. Under each control-level objective, list each of the programs

Figure 18. Control summary sheet.

	First Quarter				Second Quarter			
	Manpower (MD)	Total Expense ($000)	TUA ($000)	Contribution*	Manpower (MD)	Expense ($000)	TUA ($000)	Contribution*
I. Sales up 15%/yr.								
I-A. Group A up 20%/yr.	745	164.0	7,500	2,100	795	181.0	7,500	2,300
I-A-1. Region I Sales	150	30.0	–	600	200	41.0	–	500
I-A-2. Region II Sales	200	40.0	–	700	200	52.0	–	800
I-A-3. Region III Sales	200	42.0	–	600	200	39.0	–	700
I-A-4. Export Sales	195	52.0	–	200	195	49.0	–	300
I-B. Group B up 9%/yr.	165	26.5	20,000	5,000	560	108.0	20,125	6,000
I-B-1. Aftermarket	35	8.5	–	–	130	36.0	–	–
I-B-2. OEM	130	18.0	–	5,000	430	72.0	+125	6,000
I-C. Group C up 11%/yr.								
I-C-1.								
I-C-2.								
I-C-3.								
I-C-4.								
I-C-5.								
I-C-6.								

*All contributions for Objective I are net dollar-sales volume ($000).

that you have approved. We guessed at the beginning that you will have something like a hundred line items with two levels of subtotals. Now we are going to spread each of these line items against a time line. I suggest you do this by quarters for the first year and annually for subsequent years. You can do it in more detail if you want, but I am not sure it will tell you much more. You may not get all this on one sheet, but you can use foldouts, or cut sheets, or whatever suits your style.

For each time period there will be four columns. The first is "manpower," or I guess we should say "person power." Opposite each approved program, put the number of person-days scheduled to be devoted to that program during the time period. Count only your own people. The help you get from outside the company or from support departments within the company will be counted as a dollar expense. Some people like to use a dollar payroll expense for this kind of summarizing and in some cases it is a little more precise, but, as you will see, it will not do one of the things we hope to get out of this "people budget."

The second column, "total expense," records the program budget for that time period. Include both out-of-pocket and allocated expenses, including payrolls.

The third column, "TUA" (total utilized assets), is devoted to the area of activity the program involves. Follow your company practice with regard to capitalizing leased assets. This is a total assets figure, not new investments. Changes in this figure from time period to time period will tell you when new capitalized investments are scheduled. There are certain kinds of activities—primarily staff services—where this number has little meaning and can be eliminated, but don't overlook it too fast. If, for instance, the sales department is not charged for the investment in receivables, then somebody else had better be.

The final column in each quarter period is "contribution," or benefit, which requires some explanation and should be footnoted on the summary sheets. At the higher levels of management it can probably be stated in terms of operating income, or cash flow, or even net income. As we get down to more specialized responsibilities, the proper term may become more obscure. However, in almost all cases it can be, and should be, expressed in the terms in which the objective at the responsibility level is set, which automatically makes the figures addable, to determine whether or not the responsibility is in fact being fulfilled.

It is going to be a little tedious to fill in all these numbers, but if you will discipline yourself to do it, the summary sheets will do a number of things for you. In the first place, most of the numbers are going to come from your subordinates, extracted from their project plans. Consequently, just the existence of a blank line or a blank box tells you that someone has not done his or her homework yet, or at least that you have not approved it.

When you do have all the numbers, they give you an overall perspective on your strategic priorities. Is the distribution of your person power, or your expenses, or your investment roughly commensurate with the relative contribution you expect? If, in a certain area of responsibility, you have committed only 10 percent of your personnel resources and 30 percent of your expense budget and very little investment to a program that you expect to make 50 percent of the contribution, you may be chintzing and might just not make it. The opposite can be equally true. You may be committing a disproportionate amount of your resources to programs that you really do not expect to be vitally important to the overall objective.

The Sum of Resource Commitments

Now if you add your columns down, you will find out what your planned resource commitment is. The first one, manpower, is likely to give you the greatest shock. You know how many man-days you have available in your area of authority in a given quarter. In certain areas of responsibility you will have to exclude great blocks of time for continuing production, routine sales calls, regular administrative procedures, and so on. If the bottom line of that manpower column is more than about 75 percent of total manpower availability, you are in trouble. Remember, you have to leave slack for some slippage, for some routine administrative time, and for some short-term crises.

The expense totals for the first year should bear a pretty close relationship to your upcoming budget, and your TUA will tell you something about how your balance sheet will look. Don't worry about accounting-type accuracy in these figures. What you are after is a relative feel of the way in which you are going to distribute your resources and a check on the adequacy of those resources.

You cannot add up the contribution column because the units are not all the same.

If you want to keep a lot of supporting data, staff analyses, correspondence, historical data, and so on with your plan material, put it in a separate ring binder and organize it with the same code system you used to designate your hierarchy of objectives. If the supplementary material does not fall neatly into the objective categories, maybe there is something wrong with your information analysis system. Then again, there might be something wrong with the way that you organized your objectives.

The Comprehensive Plan

The net total of all the individual planning-control books constitutes the comprehensive plan for the company. It is a lot of paper; there is no real reason to try to put it together in a book. An open file kept in the president's office and organized according to the objective code is a lot more practical. It will not be consulted frequently, probably one when there is a breakdown in the organization somewhere, a key person leaves, or there is some other evidence that things are coming apart and someone has to go in and reconstruct the logic of the plan.

And things *will* come apart sometimes. The theory is elegantly simple. If every manager understands his or her responsibilities and accepts them honestly, guides his or her subordinates' approach to their responsibilities through the approval mechanism, and keeps on top of the key performance criteria necessary to achieve objectives, it should all add up "according to plan." It is strictly "You make your numbers, and I'll make my numbers." But unfortunately, information is sometimes faulty, judgments are frequently faulty, and sometimes— not as often as is commonly claimed, but occasionally—something does occur outside the corporation that just could not have been reasonably anticipated.

What you want is a system that will adjust to these dislocations as far down the hierarchy as possible. If performance at one of your points of control begins to drift too far off the mark, get with the person responsible for that control-level objective. Review with him or her the programs you have approved and see whether they can be modified to get the thing back on the track. If they cannot, then you may have to agree to let the person change his or her objective. Then you will have to see what you can do about shuffling your control-level objectives so that they will still add up to the objective for which you are directly responsible. You cannot change that objective without negotiations with your superior. If you cannot see a way out, you had better start negotiating.

If everybody at each level of the chain of command will manage his or her plan this way, real problems will telegraph themselves up through the system quite quickly. Minor problems will damp themselves out without involving more than two or three levels of authority.

SUGGESTED READING

Anthony, R. N., *Planning and Control Systems: A Framework for Analysis.* Boston: Harvard Business School, 1969.

The bible on the subject.

Emery, J. C., *Organizational Planning and Control Systems.* New York: The Macmillan Company, 1969.

Integrates the planning and control systems.

Tomb, J. O., "A New Way to Manage—Integrated Planning and Control," *California Management Review,* Vol. 5 (Fall 1962), pp. 57–62.

Discusses preparation of action project plans, with examples.

12
In Summary

I have thought that a man of tolerable abilities may work great changes, if he first forms a good plan and makes the execution of that same plan his whole study and business.
B. FRANKLIN

WHAT has been presented here is one way to devise a corporate strategic plan and to make it work. It is not the only way. It is not the most elegant way. It has been simplified and stripped down to make it easy to do. In the process certain subtleties and refinements have been sacrificed. However, *it will work*. It will provide a sense of direction for your organization, help you focus your energies and your resources on those areas that have the most long-term significance to the company. The refinements and the special techniques can be added later.

There is one thing that should be apparent: *Planning is not a simple linear process*. It involves making some hypothetical approximations, then seeing that the pieces fit together, and then doubling back over the previous ground to refine the details. It is a communicative process by which the responsible managers in the organization can tell each other what they think about the business and its future in a relatively structured way to assure that there is reasonable agreement as to what is being managed and to what hoped-for end. Ultimately, it is a negotiating process in which individuals come to a mutual agreement as to what are reasonable expectations and commit themselves to specific levels of accomplishment.

It also should be apparent that the planning must be done over a period of time. It cannot be done in a few days by a group of wise men assembling on a high mountain. As the plan begins to evolve, there is a continuous need for additional input information. One phase of the process leads to another which leads to another which in turn interacts with whatever has gone before. Eventually, there is a need to propagate the plans down through the levels of the organization and involve more and more people. Those people take time to assimilate the ideas and generate their contributions.

The cycle we have described covers the better part of a year. That is a good pace. It means that no sooner do you finish one cycle than you start right at the beginning of the next cycle. Don't complain that you never finish planning. That is exactly the point. Planning is not something that you do in a "season," as is the case with the budgeting period. Planning is a way of managing, and so it goes on continually just as management responsibility goes on continuously. As you go on to the second annual cycle, you will be wiser than you were in the first cycle. Not only will you have more information, but you will know more about what information you need and where to look for it. You should also have a more profound understanding of the dynamics of your company and industry and the general environment in which they operate.

Eventually, you will want to make your environmental analyses much more profound to provide greater protection against future shock as events swirl around you in an ever accelerating frenzy. You will want to formalize your planning assumptions much more than I have tried to do in this book.

As you become more skillful in the use of the planning attitude, you will plan with greater ease and subtlety. You will find eventually that you can comfortably begin to employ more of the elaborate and sophisticated techniques of planning. You will feel the need for much more sophisticated operational analysis and perhaps move toward a systems concept. You will undoubtedly computerize not only your input data analysis but eventually the planning model itself so that it will become practical to experiment with a number of alternative plans. You will be able to afford to develop one or more contingency plans—not because you will have so much more money but because you will have more time and be able to develop them faster.

You might aspire to a dynamic plan that is not produced on an annual cycle but is continually updated as new inputs become available. But don't rush it. Be sure that you are using the relatively simple basic techniques with assurance before you begin to elaborate. Your plans will change from year to year, not so much in their basic structure as in their detail. That is also as it should be. Planning is not an attempt to predict with accuracy what will happen in the future. No one is so wise as to presume such foreknowledge, and only the foolish hope that it might be possible.

A planned management is a self-conscious and self-critical management. It is a management that guides its present actions by a cold-eyed appraisal of probable future consequences. It is not a management that pretends to be inevitably right. It is a management that, through a conscious rationality, seeks to keep its mistakes small and to assure itself of the earliest possible opportunity to correct these inevitable mistakes. It seeks consistency of purpose and flexibility of action rather than thoughtless repetition of habitual actions with no clear sense of purpose at all.

A certain mystique has grown up around planning, which seems to both frighten and fascinate many managers. It frightens them because they think it employs some kind of arcane wisdom and exotic technique to which they can never aspire. It fascinates them because they feel that if once they could be initiated into the mysteries, all their problems would be solved. Neither reaction is justified.

Although planning does have its exotica, its most important contribution is in providing a disciplined, structural matrix within which to make important management decisions. It will not insure that those decisions are inevitably right. It cannot control the frustrating uncertainties of future events or completely prevent the staggering impact of occasional crises.

What it can do is provide a perspective that can assure that decisions are made in the context of the total situation, that decisions are made about the right thing and at the right time. Planning cannot predict the future, but it can provide a kind of gyroscopic stabilizer that at least provides a firm platform from which unexpected shocks can be sustained and new forays initiated.

Try it, you'll like it. For most executives, planned management is an acquired taste, but it can become addictive. It makes life so much simpler. Almost any company can make money if the management is smart enough and the people work hard enough. But there are hard ways to make money and prosper, and there are easy ways to make money and prosper. Planned management can point you to the easy way. Why do things the hard way?

SUGGESTED READING

Ackoff, R. L., *A Concept of Corporate Planning*. New York: Wiley-Interscience, 1970.

A sophisticated planning approach heavily dependent on systems analysis and mathematical models.

Anonymous, "Corporate Planning—Piercing Future Fog in the Executive Suite," *Business Week* (April 28, 1975).

Rapid changes and gross uncertainties in the business environment are leading most big companies to step up their planning activities. They are producing more alternate scenarios and multiple contingency plans, and often try to optimize strategy to straddle more than one scenario. There is a trend to shorter planning cycles with quarterly, monthly, or virtually continuous updates.

Ansoff, H. I., *Corporate Strategy*. New York: McGraw-Hill Book Company, 1965.

Strategy planning that assumes the continual necessity to change the nature of the firm. Heavy on environmental analysis and decision theory.

Starr, M. K., *Management: A Modern Approach*. New York: Harcourt Brace Jovanovich, 1971.

A total management system that starts with model building, proceeds to decision making, and then on to planning, controlling, and organizing. Very mathematical.

Index